The Artist

Since Mrs. Coucill's portraits of political figures first started appearing half a century ago, she has become one of the leading portrait artists in Canada. There must be few people in Canada who have not seen her work at one time or another, whether it was in a book, in a Hall of Fame, on the wall at a museum or perhaps on a coin or trade currency.

Born in London, Ontario in 1918 and educated in Toronto at York University, Irma Coucill started her career during the Second World War, when she was commissioned to draw portraits of personnel in the Royal Canadian Air Force, the Royal Air Force and the Norwegian Air Force.

Many other commissions have followed. When the Hockey Hall of Fame opened in 1958, Mrs. Coucill was asked to draw the portraits of all the players inducted into the Hall. The collection, housed permanently at The Great Hall, BCE Place in Toronto, has now grown to over 318 drawings, and is visited each year by thousands of sports fans.

In 1973 Mrs. Coucill was commissioned to draw portraits of the more than 160 members of Canada's Aviation Hall of Fame - the air aces of the First World War, and our intrepid bush pilots. Her 114 portraits of members of the Canadian Business Hall of Fame are displayed in BCE Place in Toronto.

With her work being published in over half a dozen books from 8 different Canadian publishers, Mrs. Coucill was also a contributing artist to the Junior Encyclopedia of Canada in 1990 and the Junior Encyclopedia of Canada CD-ROM in 1995.

The portraits of the many famous Canadians that over the years have come from her pencil have made Irma Coucill one of the most renowned interpreters of our historical personalities.

Photo by Tom Coucill

*To Pierre Elliott Trudeau
who has inspired in Canadians
the true ideal of unity*

CANADA'S PRIME MINISTERS,

Governors General and Fathers of Confederation

*Inscribed by the artist
for Bill White
with Best Wishes
for the Coming Century
and the Millennium
Irma Coucill
9/12/99*

81 Portraits by

IRMA COUCILL

with Biographies

Foreword by
Michael Bliss

Pembroke Publishers Limited

Pembroke Publishers
538 Hood Road
Markham, Ontario, Canada L3K 3K9
www.pembrokepublishers.com

Distributed in the U.S. by **Stenhouse Publishers**
P.O. Box 360
York, Maine 03909
www.stenhouse.com

This book was published in previous editions as *Founders & Guardians*.

Pembroke Publishers gratefully acknowledges the support of the Department of Canadian Heritage.

Canadian Cataloguing in Publication Data

Coucill, Irma, 1918–
    Canada's prime ministers, governors general and Fathers of Confederation

Includes index.
ISBN 1-55138-114-1

1. Prime ministers – Canada – Portraits. 2. Prime ministers – Canada – Biography. 3. Governors general – Canada – Portraits. 4. Governors general – Canada – Biography. 5. Fathers of Confederation – Portraits. 6. Fathers of Confederation – Biography. 7. Statesmen – Canada – Portraits. 8. Statesmen – Canada – Biography. I. Title.

FC25.C67 1999   971'.009'9   C99-931402-5
F1005.C67 1999

Edited and Updated by Mark Leslie Lefebvre
Design: John Zehethofer
Typesetting: JayTee Graphics

Printed and bound in Canada
0 9 8 7 6 5 4 3 2 1

Contents

Preface

In 1964 the *Toronto Star* commissioned the prominent artist Irma Coucill to execute a series of drawings of the Fathers of Confederation. Mrs. Coucill's work was already well known to Canadians, particularly readers of the *Toronto Star*, where her portraits of famous show business personalities had been appearing for several years. Her drawings of Canada's hockey greats were also on display in the Hockey Hall of Fame at BCE Place in Toronto.

The series of drawings of the Fathers of Confederation, together with brief biographies, proved immensely popular, and were later sold as a portfolio by the Toronto Star Readers Service in 1964-65.

The drawings were next used by the Ontario Department of Education as a centennial project, and an attractive portfolio, including 36 portraits and biographical material, was distributed to all Ontario schools, libraries and government offices.

In 1968, as one of the projects sponsored by the federal Centennial Commission, Irma Coucill was asked to add drawings of all the Governors General and Prime Ministers since Confederation. These drawings were published with prefaces and biographies prepared by Clyde R. Blackburn and Jean-Charles Bonenfant. The book was designed as a tribute to the Founders and Guardians of Canada during the previous century, and was dedicated to "The Guardians of the future in whom we have confidence that the second century will be greater than the first."

The collection has been revised and updated over the years and this latest edition continues to recognize our leaders' contribution to the evolving Canadian identity.

Acknowledgements

For permission to reprint previously published material the artist and publishers wish to thank the following: The Ontario Ministry of Education, The Honourable Thomas Wells, Minister, and Mr. R.A.L. Thomas, Assistant Deputy Minister; Mr. J.M. DesRoches, Deputy Minister of Supply, Department of Supply and Services.

Many people have been of great assistance to the artist in the course of her research in preparation for the drawings and the new material for this volume. In particular, sincere thanks are expressed to the following people: The Office of the Prime Minister; Mr. I. Norman Smith; Mrs. Patricia Beauchesne Forbes; the Honourable Marc Lalonde; His Grace the Duke of Devonshire; the Honourable Frank McGee; Maureen Boyd at Government House; the Public Archives of Canada; the Public Archives of Ontario; the John Ross Robertson Collection of the Metro Toronto Public Library; the Toronto Star Library; and Mrs. Betty Eligh.

Foreword

Canada means many different things to people from Newfoundland and Nova Scotia, through Quebec and Ontario, west to Alberta and British Columbia, and North to the Yukon and Nunavut. Above all Canada is a country, a federation of provinces with a national government in Ottawa that has been in place ever since the Confederation year of 1867. The most important national political leaders of Canada have been the Fathers of Confederation, who forged a new country in a time of conflict and uncertainty; the Governors-General, who as the monarch's representative in Canada have been our formal heads of state, and, above all, the Prime Ministers, who run our governments from day to day with the help of our other Members of Parliament. This book is a wonderful portrait gallery of Canada's historic political elite, a kind of pictoral Hall of Fame of Canadian politics.

The artist, Irma Coucill, is unmatched as a Canadian Hall-of-Famer in her own right. For more then forty years she has been the official portrait artist for the Hockey Hall of Fame, for twenty-five years she has drawn the members of Canada's Aviation Hall of Fame, for twenty-years the Canadian Business Hall of Fame, and recently she has added the Canadian Medical Hall of Fame. She has published several previous books and her work has appeared in most Canadian newspapers and magazines. Irma will not tell me whether Wayne Gretzky has a more interesting face than Pierre Elliott Trudeau. I think she finds all superstars fun to draw (I have never seen an artist who smiles so often when she talks about her work), and she has drawn so many of them, in so many walks of life, over so many years, that she has become a Canadian portrait superstar herself. As you leaf through these pages, getting to know Canada through the faces and biographies of many of its greatest achievers, you will see why.

Michael Bliss

Prime Ministers

Twenty prime ministers have guided Canada since Confederation. These men and women have watched the nation grow from a mere federal union of four provinces and a population of about 4 million, to ten provinces and three territories with a population of more than 30 million. Their statesmanship, foresight and dreams have yielded the many blessings we enjoy and moulded the values that the nation celebrated during its centennial year.

In 1867, the young nation, the second largest national land mass in the world, was in dire need of transportation facilities to bridge the vast distances of wilderness separating the settled communities. One hundred and thirty years later, Canadians enjoy as fine a transportation system as any in the world: modern air lines, good super-highways and secondary roads, and more railway services from coast to coast than can be economically utilized.

The prime ministers of Canada's first 130 years have witnessed and brought about many significant changes in Canada's relations with the Crown and with foreign countries. Two unprecedented World Wars occurred within a period of twenty-five years. Canada played a significant role in both conflicts, giving the best of her national resources, her youth, to the defence of democracy.

From a status only slightly removed from that of a Crown colony, Canada has emerged an autonomous nation. On April 17, 1982, this country's independence was fully recognized when the Constitution was patriated. After 115 years of confederation, Canadian parliamentarians gained the right to make amendments to their own Constitution without the assent of the British Parliament. Incorporated in the Constitution is a new Canadian Charter of Rights and Freedoms, which establishes and protects the democratic, legal and equality rights of all Canadians.

Canada's prime ministers will continue to deal with the Throne through the Governor General, who is appointed on the recommendation of the Canadian government and acts on the advice of that body.

In 1880, Canada began sending High Commissioners to London to facilitate dealings with the Westminster government.

Canada's representation abroad has grown over the years to the extent of embassies in more than 100 countries, ten high commissionerships in Commonwealth countries, and a number of legations, consulates and permanent missions in a diplomatic network involving most areas of the globe.

On July 1, 1867, amidst the splendour of the new Parliament Buildings in Ottawa, the Rt. Honourable John A. Macdonald, one of Confederation's chief architects, was informed by Viscount Monck, the Queen's representative and the first Governor General under confederation, that Her Majesty had conferred a knighthood on him and instructed him to form a government and hold immediate general elections.

From this historic date to the passing of the Constitution Act in 1982, Canada has evolved into a nation of diverse cultures that is rich in opportunity. Its story is the story of its Guardians, as related in the brief sketches on the following pages.

Sir John Alexander Macdonald

(Cons.) 1867-1873, 1878-1891

A Father of Confederation and probably its chief architect, Sir John A. Macdonald was the new nation's first prime minister and directed its destinies a total of nineteen years.

For twenty-three years before confederation he had been a powerful force in the development of the Canada of that day and it has been said the story of Sir John's adult life is the history of Canada.

Glasgow-born in 1815, he was brought to Canada at five, left school to help his family at fifteen, studied while he worked and was admitted to the bar at twenty-one. His natural gifts led him into local politics and in 1844, he won the Kingston seat for the Conservatives in the legislature of Upper Canada. Three years later he was in the cabinet and in 1857 he became Conservative leader and Prime Minister of the united Canadas.

With the co-operation from Liberal and French-Canadian leadership, he sparked into action the long-smouldering urge for provincial union of all Canada. He helped form the great coalition which went to the historic Charlottetown Conference in 1864 and started the move that never lost momentum until confederation was proclaimed July 1, 1867.

He was chosen first Prime Minister by the Queen's Canadian representative, with instructions to form a government and hold immediate general elections. His party won with 101 seats to 80 and Sir John launched the great united Canada experiment.

Manitoba in 1870, British Columbia in 1871 and Prince Edward Island in 1873 joined the charter members—Ontario, Quebec, New Brunswick and Nova Scotia. There were to be no more accessions until 1904.

British Columbia had come in with the promise of a railway linking it to the east. That promise brought the famous Canadian Pacific scandal and Sir John his most bitter political experience. Alleged political-financial misdeeds brought Sir John's resignation in 1873 and his party's defeat at the polls in 1874. He came back with a sweeping victory in 1878 and was Prime Minister until his death in 1891.

A tall, handsome man with gracious manners and a fine gift of oratory, possessed of strengths and weaknesses which endeared him to all classes, he was equally at ease in a royal palace or a humble cottage. He laid much of the foundation of the Canada of today.

Completely exhausted by the strain of winning the 1891 general election, he nevertheless insisted on presiding at the new Parliament but suffered a stroke a few weeks later and died within ten days. He is buried in Cataraqui Cemetery near Kingston.

Alexander Mackenzie

(Lib.) 1873-1878

A former stone-mason turned newspaper editor, Alexander Mackenzie faced a difficult task when called to form a government following the resignation of the Conservative administration in 1873. The new national structure was still toddling. British Columbia was threatening to secede because of the Canadian Pacific issue, which brought the Macdonald government down, and there was widespread depression.

A Scot like his predecessor, Mackenzie was born in Perthshire in 1822 and came to Canada at twenty, settling first in Kingston. He worked as a stone-mason for St. Lawrence River canals and helped to build Fort Henry. Later, he moved to Sarnia where he became interested in politics and was editor of the Lambton Shield, a Liberal organ.

A staunch ally of Liberal leader George Brown, founder of the *Toronto Globe*, Mackenzie entered the Canadian Parliament in 1861. By 1867, Brown had retired from political life and Mackenzie became party head and opposition leader in the first Parliament after confederation.

At that time he was also a member of the Ontario legislature but gave that up when dual representation was abolished in 1872. He is credited with establishing secrecy of the ballot in Canadian elections.

Sir John brought the Conservatives back with a two-to-one victory in 1878 and Mackenzie returned to opposition. Ill health forced his retirement two years later. He died in 1892.

HONOURABLE

Sir John Joseph Caldwell Abbott

(Cons.) 1891-1892

Although in political life for more than thirty years, Sir John Joseph Caldwell Abbott claimed an aversion for party politics and was a most reluctant successor when he was drafted to step into the leadership vacated by the death of Prime Minister Sir John A. Macdonald in 1891.

There were logical successors to Sir John among the Conservative giants, but for one reason or another they were not suitable choices at that moment. Abbott was quoted as saying he was chosen 'because I am not particularly obnoxious to anybody.'

Abbott served as the member for Argenteuil from 1857 to 1874 and 1880 to 1887 and was appointed to the Senate in 1887, where he became government leader. As Prime Minister, he ran his office from the Senate while John S.D. Thompson spoke for him in the House.

He was the first native Prime Minister of new Canada, born in St. Andrews, Quebec, March 12, 1821. A commercial law expert, he was Dean of Law at McGill University from 1855 to 1880 and legal adviser to the Canadian Pacific Railway from 1880 to 1887.

There were many frustrations and problems in his brief tenure, including the simmering Manitoba School question and a general depression which was again striking at the economy. He managed to get the Trade and Commerce Department organised. The enabling legislation had been passed in 1887.

Abbott's stay in the prime ministership was less than eighteen months of trouble and frustrations complicated by persistent ill health which finally forced him to retire. He lived only a few months longer, dying in 1893.

Sir John Sparrow David Thompson

(Cons.) 1892-1894

A physically and intellectually powerful man, frugal and painfully honest, dedicated to public service and especially to the judiciary, Sir John S.D. Thompson died in the prime of life when his abilities and influence were needed to mend the political fences of the Conservative party.

Born in Halifax, 1844, of Irish descent, he was called to the bar in 1865. He went to the Nova Scotia legislature for Antigonish from 1877 to 1882 in which time he was successively Attorney General and Premier. Later he became a justice of the provincial Supreme Court.

Sir John A. Macdonald called him to Ottawa as Justice Minister in 1885 and he won the federal seat in Antigonish. After Macdonald's death the government was led briefly by Sir John Abbott from his place in the Senate.

Thompson ran proceedings in the House of Commons and when Sir John Abbott resigned, Thompson became Prime Minister in fact and gave promise of being a good one, admired by his associates and respected by his political foes.

He took part on behalf of Britain in the international tribune which, at Paris, laid the foundations for settlement of fisheries rights in the Bering Sea, and he was prominent in negotiations over copyright and merchant shipping laws at an Inter-Colonial conference in London.

In 1894, just as the party was getting back into good shape, strengthened and stimulated by his leadership, word came from London that Sir John had suffered a fatal seizure in Windsor Castle, where he had gone to be honoured with membership in the Imperial Privy Council. His body was brought home for burial in Holy Cross Cemetery, Halifax.

Sir Mackenzie Bowell

(Cons.) 1894-1896

Printer's devil at eleven, owner of the *Belleville Intelligencer* weekly and its sizable printing plant at twenty-seven, Sir Mackenzie Bowell held office for about fourteen troubled months.

Born in Rickinghall, Suffolk, December 27, 1823, son of a builder who brought his family to Canada ten years later, Bowell was apprentice to the printer and publisher of the *Intelligencer.*

Sixteen years later, young Bowell owned the plant and in 1866 made the paper a daily. His conciliatory stand on religious problems and the powerful attacks of Liberal leader George Brown helped him lose his first try for the legislature in 1863.

In the 1867 general election, he went to the House of Commons from North Hastings and remained there for twenty-five years. For thirteen years he was Minister of Customs, one year as Minister of Militia and two years as Minister of Trade and Commerce.

In 1892, he reluctantly accepted appointment to the Senate and became government leader there. A year later, he made a memorable trip to Australia and laid foundations for what was to be the significant Colonial Conference of 1894.

When Sir John S.D. Thompson died suddenly December 14, 1894, there was a scurry to find a successor. When the smoke cleared, Bowell had willingly become Prime Minister.

It was not a popular choice, but Bowell, knighted in 1895, surprised his enemies and his friends alike in moments of crisis, which he handled from his place in the Senate while George E. Foster led the House. It was not a good arrangement and Sir Mackenzie Bowell resigned in 1896. The Conservatives were defeated in 1896 and Bowell was named leader of the opposition in the Senate, where he remained until his resignation in 1906.

He died at Belleville, Ontario, December 10, 1917.

Sir Charles Tupper

(Cons.) 1896

Sir Charles Tupper was Prime Minister less than three months but he brought to that office a wealth of experience gained from forty years of eventful and distinguished public service. He was seventy-five years old and Canadian High Commissioner in London when induced by his colleagues to lead the government at a time when the party's morale was low.

Born in Amherst, Nova Scotia, Sir Charles was a medical doctor when he entered provincial politics and won a memorable victory in Cumberland County. Young and inexperienced, he defeated the darling of Nova Scotians, the famous and politically powerful Liberal leader, Joseph Howe. Bitterly disappointed but statesmanlike in defeat, Howe was quoted as saying he was beaten by a man who one day would be 'leader of the Conservative party.'

Tupper became Provincial Secretary when his party gained power in 1857. He sat in opposition from 1860 to 1863. The Conservatives swept the province, 40 out of 45 seats in the 1863 election, and the following year, Tupper succeeded to the Premiership.

Tupper virtually forced confederation through the Nova Scotia legislature by virtue of a motion approving a form of Canadian union but with no reference to the resolutions on confederation. It had been fought to the bitter end in and out of the legislature, particularly by Howe.

In the provincial elections that came in 1867, only two confederationists were elected and in the first Dominion election that same year Tupper, who had entered the first Macdonald cabinet, was the only confederationist elected from Nova Scotia.

In the next sixteen years he held successive portfolios in the Macdonald government and pushed forward his numerous nation-building ideas, notably concerned with railway transportation and conciliating sectarian differences.

In 1883, he was made High Commissioner in London. In 1887, Sir John called him back to the Ministry of Finance to help with the general election that year. He stayed in office one year then returned to his London post until recalled in 1896 to help the party. He became Secretary of State.

An election was essential at once since Parliament had run its statutory course. Mackenzie Bowell resigned and Tupper became Prime Minister and fought the election which the Laurier-led Liberals won.

Sir Charles remained as opposition leader till 1900 when he retired from public life and went to England where he died in 1915 at Bexley Heath in Kent. His body was brought to Halifax and given a magnificent state funeral.

Sir Wilfrid Laurier

(Lib.) 1896-1911

Canada's first French-Canadian Prime Minister, Sir Wilfrid Laurier, had an intense belief in Canada's destiny as a great nation. He had toleration and statesmanship. He was a lawyer, a fine orator and a visionary. Tall and dignified, Laurier in his later years wore his white locks in a flowing mane. 'Follow my white plume,' he cried to youthful French Canadians in Montreal in the 1911 election campaign, quoting Henry of Navarre. But his party lost to the Conservatives.

Born in 1841 at St. Lin, Quebec, Laurier got his law degree at McGill University and started practice in Montreal. He was susceptible to pulmonary diseases. Unwell and unsuccessful in Montreal, he moved to Bois Francs country near the U.S. border in what is now Arthabaska.

In that higher and drier area he thrived. He practised law and ran a newspaper, *Le Défricheur* (The Pioneer). He went to the provincial legislature in 1871 but resigned to contest his own riding in the federal elections of 1874 which he won. He was a member of the House of Commons to the day of his death.

He was defeated in 1878 in Arthabaska but won a by-election in Quebec East that same year and represented that riding to the end. He became Liberal leader in Quebec and was Minister of Inland Revenue. He became party leader in 1887.

In 1896, the Conservative party ended its long reign and Laurier formed a Liberal government. Laurier was a Catholic but often unpopular with that church. He held moderate views and believed no church should interfere with the apparatus of government. He worked to bring unity between French and English, to define and establish Canada's place in the British family of nations and to bring what he believed to be the best kind of relations with the United States.

Laurier set up the External Affairs Department in 1909, at first an adjunct of the Prime Minister's Office. It was to grow into a vast establishment sending ambassadors and legations all over the world.

He attempted to make agreement with the United States on that country's request for a reciprocal trade agreement but partly for this and his government's stand on the naval issue, the Liberals went down to defeat in the 1911 general election and Laurier went into opposition.

He suffered a series of strokes and died in office as opposition leader at Ottawa in 1919.

Sir Robert Laird Borden

(Cons.) 1911-1920

In his own quiet way, Sir Robert Laird Borden was probably one of Canada's most widely known, effective and respected prime ministers. He led the country through the greatest war ever fought up to his time, got the support of his political enemies to weather the crisis of war and conscription, and helped to achieve Canada's acceptance as an important and independent unit in the British.family.

Sir Robert performed many services for his own country and others in significant international conferences, and led a delegation as Canadian plenipotentiary at the Versailles Peace Conference. He was decorated not only by his sovereign but by the governments of France and Belgium and was laden with academic honours from world-famed universities.

Born in the historic hamlet of Grand Pré, Nova Scotia, June 26, 1854, Borden became a successful lawyer in Halifax. He went into politics and won a Halifax seat in the House of Commons in 1896. He was defeated in 1904 but won a by-election in Carleton (Ottawa); in 1908 he ran in both Carleton and Halifax and won both but chose to represent Halifax which returned him again in 1911. In the Union Government election of 1917, he was elected in his native Kings' County.

He visited the war fronts several times. Canada's 8 million population had provided an expeditionary force of 425 000 for overseas duty. He sat with the Imperial Cabinet—the first overseas minister to be so honoured—and later became a member of the Commonwealth's Imperial War Cabinet.

An ardent imperialist, he fought reciprocity with the United States. Ill health induced him to hand over his office to Arthur Meighen in 1920. He lived in Ottawa until his death June 10, 1937. His statue, along with Macdonald's, Laurier's and those of other great Canadians, stands on Parliament Hill.

Arthur Meighen

(Cons.) 1920-1921, 1926

Arthur Meighen was one of Canada's most gifted yet most unsuccessful politicians. He was Prime Minister on two occasions for an aggregate of less than nineteen months, but was in and out of politics over a period of thirty-four years.

He was born in Perth County, Ontario, June 16, 1874 and became a Toronto barrister. In 1908, he was elected to the House of Commons for Portage la Prairie, Manitoba. He was Borden's right-hand man during and after the war years and at various times held the portfolios of Solicitor General, Secretary of State, Mines and Interior. While Prime Minister, he served as Secretary of State for External Affairs.

When Borden resigned in 1920, Meighen held office from July 10, 1920 to December 29, 1921. His party was defeated in the election of December 6, 1921 and he suffered personal defeat in Portage la Prairie which he had held since 1908. He won a seat in a by-election in Grenville in 1922 and was back in the House.

In 1925, the Conservatives made a strong come-back but Mackenzie King was able to carry on with Progressive Party support till 1926; when faced by a censure vote, he asked for dissolution of Parliament. The Governor General, Lord Byng, refused and called on Meighen who had no majority, but had courage and ingenuity.

In those days, when a member entered the ministry he had to be re-elected. If he formed a ministry, Meighen and his cabinet colleagues would be unable to sit until by-elections could be held, and defeat in the House would be certain. So he had himself sworn in and appointed a cabinet of 'acting ministers' which came to be known as 'The Shadow Government,' which he directed from a seat in the gallery, pending his own confirmation at the polls. But the government was beaten in a House vote after less than three months and in the general election that followed, Meighen was defeated in Portage la Prairie, and the Liberals again formed the government.

Meighen retired to private life in Toronto. When R.B. Bennett became leader, he appointed Meighen to the Senate in 1932 and he was government leader in that chamber. In 1941, he was lured from the Senate to again lead the Conservatives and in 1942 sought a seat in York South by-election. He was defeated by a CCF candidate, and left politics for his Toronto law practice. He died August 5, 1960.

William Lyon Mackenzie King

(Lib.) 1921-1926, 1926-1930, 1935-1948

William Lyon Mackenzie King was confederation's first bachelor Prime Minister. He was an astute politician who won record party victories at the polls. He was prime minister longer than any other British leader—a total of just over twenty-one years.

He led Canada through the Second World War and the many crises it engendered at home and abroad. He was a shy and sensitive man but could rule with an iron hand and often did. He believed it possible to communicate with the spirit world.

Mackenzie King was born December 17, 1874 in Kitchener, Ontario, grandson of the rebel leader William Lyon Mackenzie. He was educated at Toronto University, Chicago University and Harvard. He was made a C.M.G. in 1906 but always opposed the award of titular honours. Mackenzie King became Deputy Labour Minister in 1900. In 1908 he was appointed Labour Minister and entered the House of Commons. He went down with the government in the 1911 elections and was out of the House until 1919.

He succeeded Laurier as Liberal leader in 1919 and returned to the House as opposition leader. He was Prime Minister from December 29, 1921 to June 28, 1926; from September 25, 1926 to August 7, 1930 and from October 23, 1935 to November 15, 1948, when he resigned because of failing health.

Mackenzie King was elected successively in North Waterloo (1908), Prince, P.E.I. (1919), North York (1921), Prince Albert (1926, 1930, 1935 and 1940) and Glengarry in 1945. In 1940 the Liberals won a record 184 seats.

In 1926, faced with a censure vote and likely defeat in the Commons, Mackenzie King asked Governor General Byng for dissolution but His Excellency refused (thus creating the famous constitutional issue), and called on Conservative leader Meighen to attempt to form a government.

With a smaller following than King's, Meighen was defeated within three months. King fought the ensuing election on the constitutional issue, claiming that the Governor General of Canada should take his instructions from the sovereign's Canadian advisers. That point was later established beyond question.

King resigned in favour of Louis St. Laurent in 1948. He never fully regained his health and died at his country home, Kingsmere, in the Gatineau Hills near Ottawa in July 1950.

Richard Bedford Bennett

(Cons.) 1930-1935

Richard Bedford Bennett was born July 3, 1870 in Hopewell, New Brunswick. As a boy his ambition was to be a school teacher like his beloved mother and to become Prime Minister. He achieved the first ambition at eighteen but after two years decided on law which he studied at Dalhousie University. He was admitted to the New Brunswick bar in 1893.

He settled in Calgary in 1897 with the Lougheed law firm and swiftly won fame and wealth. He was in the territorial legislature before Alberta and Saskatchewan were created in 1905 and then in the Alberta legislature. In 1911 he went to the House of Commons from Calgary and was Borden's right-hand man in many critical events till 1917, when he did not seek re-election.

For a few months he was justice Minister in the first Meighen cabinet but he was defeated by 16 votes by a labour candidate in Calgary West in 1921.

Calgary West returned him in 1925, 1926, 1930 and 1935. The 1930 election, fought in the first stage of the world economic depression, brought victory to the Conservatives and to Bennett the realization of his boyhood ambition. He set to work fighting the depression in Canada.

He assumed the Finance portfolio for a year, along with that of External Affairs. In 1932, he called the Imperial Economic Conference in Ottawa, when the British preferential system of tariffs was adopted. He also founded the Central Bank. Near the end of his term, Bennett had all but concluded a reciprocal trade agreement with the United States. Bennett restored the award of titles to Canadians and several received knighthoods.

The Conservatives suffered humiliating defeat in 1935, winning only 39 seats, and Bennett went into opposition. He had been ill before the election and was still ailing. In 1937 he retired and went to England, bought an estate near Leatherhead, Surrey and was created Viscount.

Like Mackenzie King, he remained a lifelong bachelor. True to a promise given his mother, he never tasted intoxicants and never smoked, nor would he work on the Sabbath except under dire necessity.

He died suddenly at Dorking, Surrey on June 27, 1947.

Louis Stephen St. Laurent

(Lib.) 1948-1957

Following the death of his powerful Quebec lieutenant, Ernest Lapointe, Mackenzie King searched for a new Quebec leader who would be a good successor when he retired. He chose Louis St. Laurent. To the end, King talked with pride of the wisdom of his choice. He persuaded St. Laurent to give up a great law practice to become Justice Minister in December 1941.

St. Laurent looked for a seat in Quebec East which had returned Laurier in ten general elections and two by-elections, Lapointe in six general elections and three by-elections and which in time supported him in his by-election and returned him in four general elections.

St. Laurent was born February 1, 1882, in Compton, Quebec, of a French-speaking father and an English-speaking mother. He was fluently bilingual from childhood.

He graduated in law from Laval University and practised with exceptional success in Quebec. With the high respect of French Canadians, an international reputation in legal circles and a great understanding of humanity, yet with no previous political experience, St. Laurent was an immediate success in the war cabinet and thereafter.

Mackenzie King handed over the party leadership to St. Laurent in August 1948 and in November of the same year gave up the prime ministership to his chosen successor.

St. Laurent was responsible for several important departmental changes and was prominent in the field of international relations. He was one of the first western leaders to advocate the North Atlantic Treaty Organization.

St. Laurent nominated the first Canadian-born Governor General (Vincent Massey) and it was under his administration that the St. Lawrence Seaway project was finally launched in co-operation with the United States.

He won the 1949 general election, the first under his leadership, with a record 190 seats. His party was edged out in 1957 by the Conservatives under John Diefenbaker.

In early 1958, St. Laurent retired and returned to his law practice in Quebec City, where he died on July 25, 1973.

John George Diefenbaker

(Cons.) 1957-1963

Like so many who have attained high place, John Diefenbaker fixed his sights on the prime ministership when very young, and made no secret of it. He was strengthened in this ambition in a half-hour talk in Saskatoon with Sir Wilfrid Laurier, when Diefenbaker, aged fifteen, was delivering newspapers. Both were impressed with each other and Laurier was quoted by his biographer as saying that Diefenbaker was a 'remarkable newsboy.'

Born in Neustad, near Owen Sound, Ontario September 18, 1895, Diefenbaker went to Saskatchewan as a child with his farming parents. His education at the University of Saskatchewan was interrupted by service overseas as an artillery lieutenant. Invalided in 1917, he returned to university and became a lawyer.

He soon became one of Canada's best criminal lawyers and a great debater. He was always interested in politics and unsuccessfully attempted the federal riding of Prince Albert in 1925 and 1926. He was successful in Lake Centre in 1940, 1945, and 1949; he won Prince Albert in 1953 and retained this seat in subsequent elections.

He was chosen Conservative leader at a convention in Ottawa in 1956 and the following year, his party won 112 seats, more than any other group, and he formed a government. A year later he went after a better deal in the House membership and his party won 208 seats out of 245, a record that would not be surpassed until 1984.

The voters were less kind in the 1962 election and Diefenbaker, with only 116 seats, carried on with difficulty till 1963 when another general election gave the Liberals a near majority and they formed the government.

In 1965, the Liberal position improved slightly and Diefenbaker remained leader of the opposition.

One of the outstanding measures of the Diefenbaker regime was the enactment of legislation containing the Bill of Rights guaranteeing Canadians their fundamental freedoms.

Diefenbaker died on August 16, 1979, at his home in Rockcliffe Park, just outside of Ottawa. He was given a State Funeral and his body was taken by train to be buried near the Diefenbaker Centre on the Campus of the University of Saskatchewan in Saskatoon.

Lester Bowles Pearson

(Lib.) 1963-1968

When Lester Bowles 'Mike' Pearson became Prime Minister in 1963, he was probably the best-known Canadian in the capitals of the world. A background of distinguished diplomatic and foreign affairs' experience had taken him to the major world conferences of the previous twenty-five years, and he had been a leading architect of the United Nations.

Born April 23, 1897 in Newtonbrook, Ontario he obtained his B.A. at the University of Toronto and an M.A. at Oxford.

In 1915, he interrupted his undergraduate studies to enlist, and served overseas almost three years, ending as a Flying Officer in the Royal Flying Corps. He was an athlete of some distinction and never lost his avid interest in sports, particularly baseball, hockey and football.

Entering the External Affairs Department in 1928, he rose rapidly in the service. He served in the High Commissioner's Office in London and was there during the beginning of the Second World War. By 1946, he was Canadian ambassador in Washington and, looking for more worlds to conquer, decided on politics. He returned to Ottawa and was appointed Under-Secretary for External Affairs and in 1948 was given the portfolio.

He won a by-election in Algoma East and represented that riding during his political career. He went into opposition with his party in 1957 and the following year was chosen to succeed his retiring leader, Louis St. Laurent.

In 1956 he presented to the United Nations the peacekeeping formula which brought settlement of the Suez crisis and earned him the Nobel Peace Prize in 1957.

Pearson was the chief operating head of the Canadian delegation at the founding of the United Nations in San Francisco in 1945 and was President of the Seventh Session of the General Assembly. In 1955, he made a formal visit to Moscow where he was well received as head of the External Affairs Department and he laid the foundations for a new trading arrangement.

The Liberals won 129 seats in the 1963 general election and Pearson carried on with the support of some opposition groups. He tried to better his position in an election in 1965 and came out with 131 seats, less than an overall majority. One of the outstanding events of his tenure was the adoption of the new Canadian maple leaf flag replacing the red ensign.

He announced his resignation as party leader in December 1967, and at the leadership convention in April 1968, Pierre Elliott Trudeau was chosen to succeed him as leader of the party and Prime Minister.

After his retirement, Pearson devoted the few remaining years of his life to writing his memoirs, *Mike*. He died in Ottawa, December 27, 1972 and is buried in Wakefield, Quebec.

Pierre Elliott Trudeau

(Lib.) 1968–1979, 1980–1984

Pierre Elliott Trudeau burst on the political scene like no other leader before him. He had only been in the House of Commons two and a half years when he was chosen leader of the Liberal party in April 1968.

Born in Montreal on October 18, 1919, Pierre Trudeau grew up in a bilingual family. He studied law at the University of Montreal and was called to the bar in 1943. He earned a Master of Arts degree from Harvard University and went to Europe for post-graduate work at the Ecole des Sciences Politiques in Paris and the London School of Economics.

Back in Canada, Trudeau accepted a position as desk officer in the Privy Council Office in Ottawa and in 1952 he returned to Montreal to practise law, specializing in labour law and civil liberties cases.

In 1961 Trudeau was appointed associate professor of law at the University of Montreal until his entry into federal politics in the general election of 1965.

Trudeau's parliamentary career took off auspiciously with his appointment as Parliamentary Secretary to Prime Minister Pearson in 1966. After Pearson's resignation in 1967, Trudeau stood as a candidate in the leadership convention of April 1968. His campaign fascinated Canadians and inspired the media term 'Trudeaumania'. He was voted leader on April 6, and became Canada's fifteenth Prime Minister.

On April 23 he dissolved Parliament and called a general election, which resulted in the first majority government since 1958. The subsequent election in 1972, resulted in the fifth minority government since Confederation. Defeated by a non-confidence motion in May 1974, Trudeau's Liberals returned to power in July with a comfortable majority.

With the expiry of the government's mandate in May 1979, a general election was called. On May 22, 1979 Pierre Trudeau suffered his first defeat as Leader of the Liberal Party. He tendered his resignation as Leader in November of the same year, but upon the fall of the Conservative government over their budget proposals in December, consented to return, to guide his party through the upcoming election. In February 1980, the Liberals swept to a stunning majority victory after serving only seven months as the Official Opposition.

On November 5, 1981, the provinces and the federal government reached an historic agreement over the patriation and substance of the Canadian Constitution. On April 17, 1982, the Constitution, with its endorsement of the Canadian Charter of Rights and Freedoms, was brought home.

The repatriation of the Constitution is perhaps the crowning achievement of Pierre Elliott Trudeau, a man of unique style and intellect, who has dedicated more than a decade to the political life of his country. He retired from politics in 1984 and resides in Montreal.

Joseph Clark

(Cons.) 1979-1980

Member of Parliament for Yellowhead, Alberta, Charles Joseph Clark was only forty when he and his Conservative party put a temporary end to eleven years of Liberal rule under Pierre Trudeau. His own mandate to govern was terminated six months later, when his minority government was voted out of power.

Joseph Clark was born in High River, Alberta, on June 5, 1939, son of a newspaper editor, Charles Clark, of High River, and Grace (Welch) Clark of Wainwright, Alberta.

In 1959, while still an undergraduate at the University of Alberta, Joe Clark acted as private secretary to then Alberta P.C. leader, W.J.C. Kirby. He received the Bachelor of Arts degree in History in 1960, and returned to the University of Alberta in 1965 as a lecturer in Political Science. During this time he also worked as a journalist for the CBC, the Calgary Herald and the Edmonton Journal.

Defeated as a candidate in the 1967 Alberta provincial election, he spent the next three years as Executive Assistant to national P.C. leader The Hon. Robert Stanfield.

On October 30, 1972, Clark was first elected to the House of Commons as M.P. for Rocky Mountain. On February 22, 1976, four years after his first appearance in national Parliament, he emerged from relative obscurity to be elected national leader of the Progressive Conservative Party of Canada. In spite of his years of political activity, Clark was largely unknown to the Canadian public.

In the 1979 spring election, Clark's Conservative platform included tax and mortgage breaks and a proposal to sell Petro Can, Canada's national gas and oil company, to private interests. The May 22nd election saw a Conservative victory, and Clark formed a minority government.

On December 13, 1979, the government fell after a vote of non-confidence following the introduction of a controversial, hard-line budget. The crucial issues facing Clark's government—energy policy and Quebec separatism—were still unresolved, and the important mortgage interest credit bill was still before the House.

Back on the campaign trail, Clark's platform varied little from that of the previous election. On February 18, 1980, Trudeau's Liberals came back to power with a majority. Clark was re-elected M.P. for Yellowhead, but his party won only 128 seats in Parliament. Clark continued as Leader of the Opposition, until 1983. He retired from politics in 1993 but in 1998 he was selected once again as the P.C. national leader.

John Napier Turner
(Lib.) 1984

John Napier Turner was born on June 7, 1929 in Richmond, Surrey just outside of London England. When his father died three years later, Turner's mother, who was Canadian, returned to her home town of Rossland, B.C. and was soon offered a job with the Tariff Board in Ottawa.

John Turner attended Ashbury College and St. Patrick's before his mother married a wealthy Vancouver businessman by the name of Frank MacKenzie Ross. When the family moved again, Turner enrolled at the University of British Columbia and studied political science, economics and English. He won a Rhodes Scholarship upon graduating in 1949 and studied law at Oxford. From there he went to Paris to work on a doctorate at the University of Paris. In 1953, he returned to Canada, where he joined the law firm of Stikeman and Elliott. In 1954 he was called to the Quebec Bar.

Liberal Cabinet Minister C.D. Howe lured Turner into politics in 1957 by asking him to help in the election campaign. In 1962 Turner was nominated in the St-Laurent-St-Georges riding and won the election in June.

Turner joined Prime Minister Lester Pearson's Cabinet in 1965 as Minister without Portfolio and in 1967 was made Minister of the newly-created portfolio of Consumer and Corporate Affairs.

When Pearson retired in 1968, Turner entered the leadership race, lost to Pierre Trudeau, and was made Minister of Justice, where he spent four years reorganizing and updating the department. In 1972 he became Minister of Finance and held that post until he resigned in 1975 and left politics the following year to join the Toronto law firm of McMillan Binch.

Turner remained in private practice until Trudeau retired in 1984. Turner successfully ran for leader of the Liberal party and became Prime Minister on June 30, 1984. Without a seat in the House of Commons, and gambling on his new popularity as leader, Turner called an early election and was severely defeated.

As leader of the Opposition, Turner took advantage of scandals and difficulties plaguing the Conservatives to rebuild the Liberal party. He used the Liberal majority in the Senate to force an election on the issue of the Free Trade Agreement in 1988. The Conservatives won the election to form a majority government, and early in 1989, Turner announced plans to step down as leader. Turner was succeeded by Jean Chrétien in June 1990.

Martin Brian Mulroney

(Cons.) 1984-1993

Ensuring that Canada was able to compete on a world market was the most important concern to Brian Mulroney. In his nine years in office, Mulroney brought in two free trade agreements, an acid rain treaty with the United States, introduced the Goods and Services Tax, set in motion the Nunavet Settlement Agreement and won respect around the world for his stand on South African Apartheid.

Martin Brian Mulroney was born in Baie-Comeau, Quebec on March 20 in 1939. He was educated at St. Francis Xavier University in Antigonish, Nova Scotia, studying arts and commerce before majoring in political science. He graduated with Honours in 1959 and studied law at Dalhousie University in Halifax before transferring to Laval University in Quebec City in 1960. He was called to the Quebec Bar in 1965 after being offered a position with the prestigious law firm of Howard, Cate, Ogilvy et al in Montreal.

Mulroney became well known in Quebec with a high-profile report he filed as commissioner in the Cliché Commissions of Inquiry into the Quebec construction industry, which uncovered unprecedented corruption and violence.

In 1976, Mulroney ran for federal leadership of the Conservative party, losing to Joe Clark on the third ballot. Shortly after the convention, he accepted an offer for the position of Executive Vice President of the Iron Ore Company of Canada, and was appointed to President the following year.

He ran again for Conservative leadership in 1983 as the only bilingual candidate, won the leadership of the Opposition, defeating Joe Clark on the fourth ballot and gained his first seat in the House of Commons through a by-election in the Maritime riding of Central Nova. In 1984, Mulroney led the Conservatives to the greatest majority in Canadian history, winning 211 seats in the House of Commons. Another majority was won in 1988.

Mulroney attempted to secure Canadian economic success by access to foreign markets through the 1988 Free Trade Agreement with the United States and the North American Free Trade Agreement with the U.S. and Mexico in 1992.

During his term, Mulroney also endeavoured to end Quebec's boycott of the 1982 constitutional reform through the Meech Lake Accord which was not ratified by all provinces by the June 1990 deadline. The Charlottetown Accord proposal was introduced in another attempt to secure constitutional unanimity, but was ultimately defeated in a national referendum on October 26, 1992.

Mulroney announced his intention to retire in February 1993 and resigned from politics on June 25, 1993. He resides in Montreal, practises law and serves on the boards of many organizations.

A. Kim Campbell

(Cons.) 1993

Being Canada's first female Prime Minister wasn't the only first for Kim Campbell. Her entry into politics at the Prince of Wales Secondary School saw her elected as the first female student council president. And she was also elected the first female freshman president at U.B.C. Years later, she became Canada's first female Justice Minister. Yet, despite her pioneering ability and her talk about a style of government called the "politics of inclusion," she served for only a brief period.

Avril Phaedra Douglas Campbell was born March 10, 1947 in Port Alberni, B.C. Shortly after, her family moved to Vancouver and she changed her name to Kim. In 1964, she went to U.B.C. and majored in political science. After graduating, she won a scholarship to the London School of Economics where she began a doctorate in Soviet studies. In 1973, with an unfinished thesis, she returned to Vancouver and began lecturing at Simon Fraser University and Vancouver Community College.

In 1980, she returned to U.B.C. to study law and was elected to the Vancouver School Board where she served for four years. In 1985 she was offered a position as a policy advisor to B.C. Socred Premier Bill Bennett. Campbell ran for provincial leader in 1986 when Bennett resigned and won a seat in the legislature. The federal Conservative party began wooing her as a candidate for the seat Pat Carney was going to be retiring from in 1988. Campbell ran and won in the 1988 election.

In 1989 she was offered a junior Cabinet post as Minister of State for Indian and Northern Affairs and in 1990 she became Justice Minister. In the wake of the 1989 Montreal massacre, she introduced a bill amending the gun laws that satisfied the public outcry for more restrictions. She also introduced Bill C-49 which focused on the principle of consent in sexual assault and which passed second reading with a rare vote of unanimity by all three federal parties.

In 1993, Campbell became Minister of National Defence and ran for party leader when Brian Mulroney announced his retirement. She beat Jean Charest in a close contest in June and became Prime Minister. At the time, the Conservative mandate to govern had expired and Campbell had to call an election in October 1993. She bore the brunt of voter's dissatisfaction over free trade, GST and the economic recession which were part of her party's nine year legacy. The Conservative party suffered an extraordinary loss, being reduced to just two seats. Losing her own Vancouver seat, Campbell retired from politics completely and returned to her studies, accepting a fellowship at Harvard.

On September 16, 1996, she was appointed Consul General for Canada in Los Angeles.

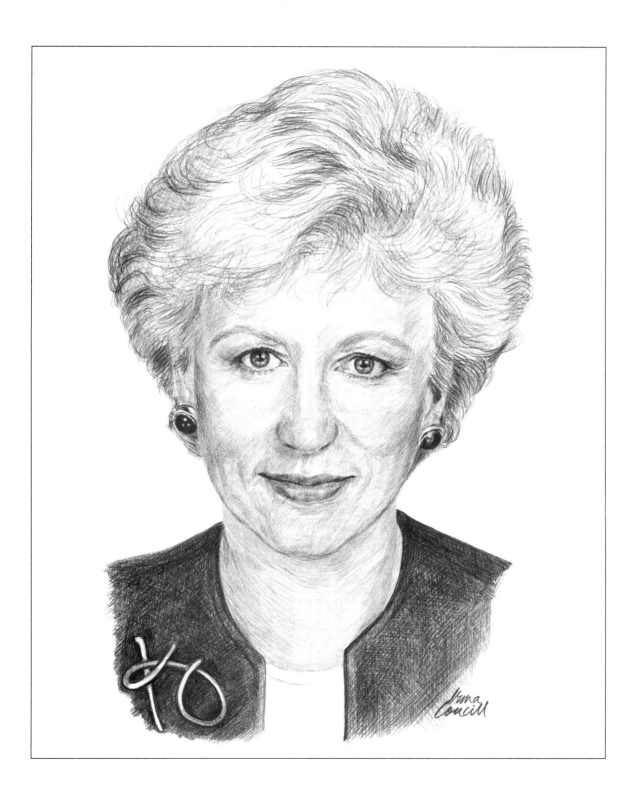

Jean Chrétien

(Lib.) 1993 -

Canada's twentieth Prime Minister, Joseph Jacques Jean Chrétien, was born on January 11, 1934 in Shawinigan, Quebec, the same day as Sir John A. Macdonald. He has served with six prime ministers, held twelve ministerial positions and sat in Parliament for a total of twenty-seven years, making his long years of experience his greatest asset as a Prime Minister.

Educated at St. Joeseph Seminary in Trois-Riviéres, Chrétien studied law at Laval University, was called to the Bar in 1958, and set up a law practice in the working-class district of Shawinigan North.

Having been interested in politics from an early age, assisting his father as a Liberal organizer and joining the campus Liberal Club at Laval, Chrétien spent his first two years in Ottawa as a backbencher not learning the political process, but instead developing his English language skills.

Prime Minister Lester Pearson recognized Chrétien's enthusiasm and work ethic and made him a parliamentary secretary in 1965 working under Finance Minister Mitchell Sharp. In 1968, Prime Minister Pierre Trudeau made Chrétien Minister of National Revenue where he served briefly before moving on to Minister of Indian and Northern Affairs. During his six years as Minister, he established an office for the settling of native land claims and created ten new national parks.

In 1974, Chrétien served as President of the Treasury Board, in 1976 moved to Industry, Trade and Commerce, and then became Minister of Finance in 1977. In 1980, Chrétien became Minister of Justice and was responsible for supporting the "no" movement in the Quebec Referendum on Sovereignty. Chrétien drafted the passage of the 1982 Charter of Rights as Minister for Constitutional Negotiations.

Chrétien ran for leadership of the Liberal party in 1984 when Trudeau resigned, and lost in a close vote to John Turner. He then served as Deputy Prime Minister before resigning from politics in 1986 and returning to the practice of law.

When Turner left politics in 1990, Chrétien announced his candidacy for Liberal party leader, won the convention on the first ballot and set about rebuilding the divided and demoralized Liberal party. In 1993, the Liberals won a majority of 176 seats and on November 4, 1993, Jean Chrétien was sworn in as Prime Minister.

In another similarity to Canada's first Prime Minister, Chrétien's prime ministership faced an official opposition of separatists in Parliament. While John A Macdonald faced Nova Scotian separatists and Chrétien faced Bloc Québécois, both leaders exhibited a belief in a united Canada held together by a strong central government.

Governors General

The Governor General and Commander-in-Chief in Canada is the personal representative of the Sovereign. Our Sovereign is the Sovereign of the United Kingdom and of other member nations of the Commonwealth.

The Governor General is appointed by the Sovereign on the recommendation of the Canadian government in power, when a new appointment is necessary. The purpose of the office is obvious in the fact that our Sovereign resides elsewhere. In Ottawa the Governor General acts in the Sovereign's stead.

In simple fact the Governor General takes instructions from the Prime Minister of the day, just as the Sovereign in London depends entirely on the advice of the politicians in power at Westminster. Nevertheless, up to the present, our Governors General have been people of great knowledge and experience in diplomacy and politics, in war or in business.

Thus, while obliged to take their advice and instructions from the government of the day, through the Prime Minister, they have always been a source of good counsel and guidance to every government leader no matter how astute that official might have been.

In 1926, it was ruled beyond question that they should act only on the advice of the Sovereign's Canadian Ministry, and since then the Governor General has had no dealings with the British government. They are the channel for communications between the Prime Minister and the Throne, and their relations are solely with the Sovereign.

Normal tenure of office is about five years, but extensions of a year or two are frequent. The first pre-confederation Governor, Samuel de Champlain, held office twenty-seven years. The shortest tenure was that of Lord Durham in 1838—a total of five months. He resigned in a quarrel with his home government but left a lasting and significant document, the *Durham Report,* which brought union of Upper and Lower Canada in 1840-41 and nourished the seeds that brought the larger union in 1867.

The Governor General opens Parliament in the name of the Sovereign, dissolves it when this becomes advisable and signs all orders-in-council. In a public ceremony in the Senate Chamber, he gives Royal Assent to bills passed in Parliament, signs commissions and high appointments, and is a confidant and advisor to the Prime Minister of the day. They are also the official host to visiting heads of state and even lesser dignitaries.

The first seventeen Governors General since confederation were peers: eight English, five Irish and four Scots. The last five have been Canadian commoners.

We are presenting here brief biographies of the Governors General since confederation. It will be seen that they were all leaders of exceptionally high calibre from every viewpoint. Space permits only a brief reference to themselves and the events they helped shape in Canada.

Lack of space also prevents much reference to the galaxy of great personages who were the thirty-nine pre-confederation governors, from Samuel de Champlain (1608) to Viscount Monck (1861). They were bold, daring and adventurous men who left comfortable lives in France or Britain for the certain hardships and dangers of the new world.

The Governor General is entitled to 'Excellency.' The Governor General may not enter the House of Commons but goes to the Senate for formal occasions such as the Opening of Parliament and giving Royal Assent.

Viscount Monck

(1867-1868)

Viscount Monck was the first Governor General after confederation, and might properly be called a Father of Confederation. He had been Governor of the old Canada since 1861 and worked closely with the Fathers. Canadian historian W.L. Morton called him a 'grave, persistent architect of Confederation.'

Sir Charles Stanley, fourth Viscount Monck, was born October 10, 1819, at Templemore, Tipperary, Ireland, and was educated in law at Trinity College, Dublin. Barred, as Irish peers were, from a seat in the House of Lords, he won a House of Commons seat in Portsmouth in 1852, and later became Lord of the Treasury.

In 1861, Queen Victoria appointed Monck as 'Our Captain-General and Governor-in-Chief in and over ... all our provinces in North America and of the Island of Prince Edward.' He did everything possible to further the aspirations of the confederationists. His term normally would have expired in 1866, but he wanted to see the new Dominion established and the Queen extended his tenure.

Thus Monck was sworn in on Parliament Hill in Ottawa, July 1, 1867, as Canada's first Governor General. His first official duty was to inform Sir John A. Macdonald that the Queen had made him a Knight of the Bath, and his ministerial associates Commanders of the Bath, and that Sir John was to form a government.

Since 1866, Canada's capital had been in Ottawa and the Governor General lived in Rideau Hall down river from the office on Parliament Hill. In the summer, Monck would make the journey to his office by longboat, manned by Royal Navy bluejackets.

Monck ended his term November 14, 1868 and went home to Ireland. For his work in Canada, he was made a peer of the United Kingdom, Baron Monck of Ballytrammon, and from 1874 to 1893 he was Lord Lieutenant of the County of Dublin. He died in 1894.

Lord Lisgar

(1869-1872)

Sir John Young, baronet (later Baron Lisgar) was the second Governor General after confederation and like his predecessor was an Irish nobleman and a lawyer. Like Viscount Monck, he had once held a British cabinet post as a Lord of the Treasury and he later became Secretary to the Treasury. He acquired a broad experience in the administration of British interests in Ireland, the Ionian Islands and as Governor General of New South Wales. The town Young, N.S.W. was named in his honour.

Born in Bombay, August 31, 1807, he was the son of an Irish baronet whose seat was Baillieborough Castle, County Cavan. He studied at Lincoln's Inn and was admitted to the bar in 1834. From 1831 to 1855 he sat in the House of Commons for County Cavan. Assuming office in Canada on February 2, 1869, Sir John gave some the impression that he believed confederation would inevitably mean the separation of this country from the Empire, in favour of the United States. If so, he was soon disillusioned.

He was an able administrator but not ostentatious. He made many friends and committed few errors. He was happily and continuously surprised by the vigour and vision of Canadians and their development plans.

Many eventful occasions marked his term of office. One of the most pleasant of these was playing host to the youthful son of Queen Victoria, Prince Arthur of Connaught who, 41 years later, was to become Canada's tenth Governor General.

There had been some disappointment in Ottawa that the second Governor was a 'mere baronet' having had a Viscount for the first. But the Canadian government had reduced the amount of compensation paid to the Governor General and apparently there was little competition for the job.

However, while in office, Sir John was elevated to the peerage as Baron Lisgar of Lisgar and Baillieborough. He left Canada in June 1872 and died at his Irish home in 1876.

Earl of Dufferin

(1872-1878)

Frederick Temple Hamilton-Temple Blackwood, Canada's third Governor General, was one of the most popular and gifted men ever to hold the office.

A handsome, eloquent statesman and an Irish aristocrat, the 1st Marquis of Dufferin and Ava was born in Florence, Italy, June 21, 1826, the son of the 4th Baron of Dufferin. His mother, Selina Sheridan, Lady Dufferin, was a granddaughter of Richard Brinsley Sheridan, the playwright. He was educated at Eton and Oxford, specialized in the classics and became fluent in Latin, Greek, French and Persian as well as his mother tongue. He chose a public career and in 1849 was appointed Lord-in-Waiting to the Queen. A year later he was made a peer of the United Kingdom and took his seat in the House of Lords. He travelled widely and his impressions of the Arctic were recorded in a popular book, *Letters from High Latitudes.*

He was appointed Governor General in 1872 and shortly after travelled to every accessible part of Canada, initiating a tradition that has been followed by his successors. Often he travelled on horseback and by canoe.

On his own initiative Dufferin broke a delicate impasse by commuting the death sentence passed on Louis Riel's chief aide, Lépine. In 1876, when British Columbia was threatening to secede over the delay in obtaining a railway, he visited the province and charmed its government into patience and adherence to the federal union. He again resorted to charm and diplomacy in 1875 in Quebec, when the city planned to raze historic sites, including the old ramparts. As a result of his influence, new plans were drawn up and the walls have been preserved to this day. In recognition of his efforts, the city named a delightful promenade on the heights the Dufferin Terrace.

Upon his return to England in 1878, Dufferin served as ambassador to Russia and Turkey; headed a mission to Cairo; was Viceroy of India; ambassador to France and Italy.

He retired at the age of seventy in 1896 and died in 1902 at Clandeboye, his family seat near Belfast.

Marquis of Lorne

(1878-1883)

Canada's fourth Governor General was John Douglas Sutherland Campbell, Marquis of Lorne. A Scot, in contrast to his three Irish predecessors, he was the son and heir of the 8th Duke of Argyll, head of the powerful Campbell clan.

He was born on August 6, 1845 at Stafford House, London, the son of a prominent author and politician, and received his education at Edinburgh Academy, Eton, St. Andrews and Cambridge University. In 1868 he entered the House of Commons for Argyllshire and became private secretary to his father, the Secretary of State for India. In 1871, he married Princess Louise, the fourth daughter of Queen Victoria.

In 1878, at the age of thirty-three, the young Marquis came to Canada as Governor General. The appointment caused anxiety in some Ottawa circles, as it was felt that having a princess at Rideau Hall would result in a stiffly formal royal court. They were soon reassured however. The princess, a sculptress of some note, an artist and a writer, was as informal and friendly as her husband. They fished and played outdoor games, entertained informally and kept protocol to the essential minimum.

In 1881, the Marquis undertook a tour of 13 000 kilometres from Halifax to Fort Macleod in Alberta. He was soon able to talk publicly and with great familiarity of places and peoples in Canada about which his listeners would know very little.

Interested in literature and the arts, he founded the Royal Society of Canada, promoted the Royal Canadian Academy of Art and the National Gallery in Ottawa for which he selected the first collection of pictures which now is housed in a building bearing his name. He wrote much prose and verse about Canada.

Returning to England in 1883, he entered the House of Commons, and in 1900 he succeeded to the dukedom. He died in 1914.

Marquis of Lansdowne

(1883-1888)

Henry Charles Keith Petty- Fitzmaurice, 5th Marquis of Lansdowne and a member of the Irish nobility, was Canada's fifth Governor General after confederation and the fourth Irishman to be so honoured.

Lansdowne was born in 1845 and was educated at Eton and Oxford. He succeeded to the title at twenty-one and immediately became active in the House of Lords. At twenty-six, he was appointed a Lord of the Treasury and served as Under-Secretary for War from 1872 to 1874. He was named Secretary for India in 1880, but resigned this post following a difference with Gladstone over Irish Home Rule.

Appointed Governor General in 1883, his tenure was relatively uneventful, despite the tensions of the Riel Rebellion. An ardent fisherman and outdoorsman, he enjoyed fishing in New Brunswick, and it is recorded that in four seasons, he had taken 1245 salmon.

He travelled twice to the West Coast. His first visit was largely by primitive means of travel and he visited many Indian tribes and witnessed their rituals. In contrast, his second trip was by way of the new Canadian Pacific Railway and he thus became the first Governor General to use the line all the way.

Returning to England in 1888, Lansdowne was at once appointed Viceroy of India, where he served until 1893. He turned down the ambassadorship to Russia and served in various cabinet posts. He was War Secretary when the South African War broke out and took some of the blame for Britain's ill preparedness.

Later, he served as Foreign Secretary for five years and leader of the Unionist opposition in the House of Lords. He joined the wartime coalition government without portfolio, but resigned in 1917 and led a group seeking to promote overtures for peace with Germany. He died in 1927 at his daughter's home near Clonmel in Tipperary.

Lord Stanley

(1888-1893)

Every Canadian sports enthusiast probably knows about the Stanley Cup, the trophy fought for annually by the teams of the National Hockey League. It is also probable that few of them realize the source of the trophy. It was presented by Canada's sixth Governor General, Frederick Arthur Stanley, son of the 14th Earl of Derby and himself a baron.

Born in London in 1841, the sports loving Englishman was educated at Eton and the Military College. He was commissioned in the Grenadier Guards, but shortly after chose politics as a career. He entered the House of Commons and served in several cabinet posts, including that of Secretary of State for the Colonies.

When appointed Governor General in 1888, he found Canada much to his liking and promptly established his own fishing camp, 'Stanley House' on Baie des Chaleurs in New Brunswick, close to the salmon waters of the Cascapedia.

Travelling across the country by train, on horseback and over its waterways, Lord Stanley particularly enjoyed meeting the Indians; the rugged scenery of the Rockies held a special appeal for him.

His term of office was uneventful. He became a close friend of Sir John A. Macdonald and was particularly solicitous of the Prime Minister's failing health. Both Sir John and his main political foe, Alexander Mackenzie, died within a year of each other during Lord Stanley's tenure of office.

He returned to England in 1893 and succeeded to the title of 16th Earl of Derby. He served in a number of high public offices and died at his country seat, Knowsley, Lancashire, on June 14, 1908. He was succeeded by his son.

Lord Aberdeen

(1893-1898)

It has been said that no previous occupants of Rideau Hall had reached so deeply into the hearts and lives of the Canadian people as Lord Aberdeen and his countess, the vivacious and able daughter of the 1st Lord Tweedmouth.

John Campbell Hamilton-Gordon, the seventh Governor General, was born in Edinburgh, August 3, 1847, the second son of the 5th Earl of Aberdeen. He became 1st Marquis of Aberdeen and Temair and succeeded to the earldom on the death of his brother George, the 6th Earl.

Active in the House of Lords and one of Gladstone's staunch supporters, he served the government in several major posts and in 1886 was named Lord Lieutenant of Ireland.

To Lord Aberdeen, the appointment as Governor General in 1893 meant a return to familiar land, having come here four years earlier and established a 480-acre fruit ranch at Vernon, B.C.

Lord and Lady Aberdeen travelled extensively to all parts of the country and took an active interest in numerous welfare and cultural activities.

In 1894, the Second Colonial Conference was held in Ottawa. A forerunner of the Imperial Conferences, the discussions produced, among other things, the finalizing of plans for laying the Canada-Australia cable, which was completed in 1902.

Aberdeen caused some controversy in government circles, when in 1896 he refused to approve a list of Senate, judicial and other appointments submitted by Sir Charles Tupper. He upheld his decision on the grounds that having been defeated by Laurier, the outgoing Prime Minister did not enjoy the confidence of the electorate to make these appointments.

Financially embarrassed by the heavy expenses of office and losses incurred by his fruit ranch, Aberdeen returned to England before the expiry of his term. He was re-appointed Lord Lieutenant of Ireland and held this post for ten years. He died March 7, 1934.

Earl of Minto

(1898-1904)

Another Scot, a dashing soldier and skilled horseman, Gilbert John Murray-Kynnymond Elliot, Lord Melgund and 4th Earl of Minto, was the eighth Governor General.

He was born in London on July 9, 1845 into a family long identified with British public service. He received his education at Eton and Cambridge but decided on a military career and joined the Scots Guards in 1867. He saw service in the Russo-Turkish War in 1877; the Afghan War in 1879 and in Egypt in 1882.

An ardent horseman, he rode in the Grand National four times, and in 1874 won the French Grand National.

His appointment as Governor General in 1898 meant a return to familiar surroundings. He had served at Rideau Hall as Military Secretary to Lord Lansdowne, helped to raise the Canadian contingent of woodsmen and voyageurs for the Sudan in 1884 and in 1885 was aide-de-camp to General Middleton in the expedition to suppress the Riel Rebellion in Manitoba.

Many significant events occurred during his term, such as the South African War, the death of Queen Victoria, and the Canadian tour of the Duke and Duchess of York (later King George V and Queen Mary), during which the royal guests were escorted everywhere by Lord and Lady Minto. In 1902, Lord Minto led a great Canadian contingent of politicians and military personnel to Edward VII's coronation. Their Excellencies founded the Minto Skating Club in Ottawa, which is still active today.

When Minto first left Canada in 1885, Sir John A. Macdonald forecast that he would return some day as Governor General. When he left in 1904, Sir Wilfrid Laurier commented that he came to office untrained in constitutional practice but 'became an efficient Governor, if sometimes very stiff.'

Minto returned to England in 1904, was appointed Viceroy to India in 1905 and made a Knight of the Garter in 1910. He died in 1914.

Earl Grey

(1904-1911)

Albert Henry George Grey, 4th Earl Grey and Canada's ninth Governor General, was no stranger to the public service.

Born in St. James's Palace, London, on November 28, 1851, he was the son of the Hon. Sir Charles Grey, a private secretary to Queen Victoria for many years, and a grandson of a former British Prime Minister.

He attended Harrow and Trinity College, Cambridge and began his public life as a member of the House of Commons, then entered the House of Lords when he succeeded to the earldom on the death of a childless uncle.

A strong Empire supporter, he visited the British possessions extensively and was a close friend of Cecil Rhodes, the South African statesman and developer, who appointed him Commissioner of Rhodesia.

In 1904, he was named Governor General to succeed his brother-in-law, Lord Minto, and accepted the post eagerly. Following what had become a tradition, Grey and his countess travelled widely throughout Canada and also made many successful goodwill trips to the United States.

Lord Grey was deeply interested in the conservation and development of our forest wealth and in penal reform. He had an abounding faith in the future of Canada and predicted that it would have a population of 80 million before the end of the century.

An ardent sports fan, Earl Grey instituted the Grey Cup, which remains emblematic of senior football supremacy in Canada. He was prominent in the elaborate celebration of the 300th anniversary of the founding of Quebec City and influenced the decision to have the 1759 battlefield designated as a national park. He also contributed to the preservation of other historical sites.

Because of his popularity and at his own wish, Grey's term was extended in 1909, and he remained in Canada almost seven years. Returning to England in 1911, he devoted himself to various social works and died at Howick in 1917.

The Duke of Connaught

(1911-1916)

When the Duke of Connaught took office as Canada's tenth Governor General in 1911, he became the first member of the royal family to occupy the post.

The third and last surviving son of Queen Victoria, H.R.H. the Duke of Connaught and Strathearn was born May 1, 1850 on the 81st birthday of the Duke of Wellington, one of his godfathers from whom he took his first name, Arthur.

Destined for the Army, he received his education at the Royal Military College at Woolwich, served in Egypt and rose to the rank of general in 1893. He occupied senior army training posts on the home front, saw service in Ireland, was Inspector General of the Imperial Forces, and in 1907 was Commander-in-Chief of the Mediterranean area.

The Duke was no stranger to Canada. He had served with the Royal Marines in Montreal in 1870 and had taken part in the suppression of the Red River uprising of that year. Port Arthur, Ontario, had been named in his honour and in 1890 he travelled across Canada on his return journey from India.

The family, including his daughter, the charming Princess Patricia, was interested in many activities, particularly horsemanship. During a visit to Montreal the Duke presented the Connaught Cup for competition in the Montreal Horse Show, and to this day the award is still a coveted trophy.

His term of office was troubled by the outbreak of the First World War, but his military background enabled him to offer valuable and enthusiastic support to Canada's war effort. He helped to organize the second expeditionary force and the Canadian Patriotic Fund. Princess Patricia lent her patronage to the raising of a regiment and within sixteen days a full complement had been recruited. She presented the regiment with colours made by herself, bearing the gold monogram 'PP' on one side. The Princess Pats went on to make military history by their exploits and heroism.

On his return to England in 1916, the Duke resumed his military service and fulfilled many royal functions. He died on January 16, 1942.

Duke of Devonshire

(1916-1921)

When appointed to Canada, the eleventh Governor General, Victor Christian William Cavendish, was the 9th Duke of Devonshire, having succeeded to the title in 1908 on the death of his uncle.

Born on May 31, 1868, the son of Lord Edward Cavendish, he became known as England's richest peer and largest landowner. He was a son-in-law of former Governor General Lord Lansdowne.

Before succeeding to the dukedom he held a seat in the House of Commons and later held successive cabinet posts. He was Civil Lord of the Admiralty from 1915 to 1916.

Sworn in as Governor General on November 11, 1916, Devonshire immediately entered into the economic and social life of the Dominion and travelled extensively. He displayed a great interest in land development, farming and housing.

Many issues of great importance transpired during his term of office. Sir Robert Borden formed the coalition government, which instituted compulsory military service, and gave the vote to all who served with the armed services. In the general election of 1917, women were also granted the right to vote for the first time.

In 1921, Devonshire travelled to England to attend the marriage of his daughter, Lady Dorothy Cavendish to Captain Harold Macmillan, who would later become Prime Minister of the United Kingdom.

In 1919 he entertained the Prince of Wales and when his term ended in July 1921, he returned home to be successively appointed Secretary of the Colonies, Lord Lieutenant of Derbyshire, Chancellor of Leeds University and High Steward of Cambridge University.

The Duke died at his estate, Chatsworth, in Derbyshire May 6, 1938.

Lord Byng

(1921-1926)

Julian Hedworth George Byng, Canada's twelfth Governor General, brought to his office a distinguished military record. Born on September 11, 1862, the son of the 2nd Earl of Strafford, he became a professional soldier and served in India, in the South African War, with the occupation forces in Egypt and in the First World War. He commanded an army corps in the ill-fated Dardanelles campaign and supervised the evacuation from the Straits.

In May 1916, Byng was given command of the Canadian Corps in France and led them in the capture of Vimy Ridge. At the end of the war, in recognition of his outstanding leadership and service, he was created baron. He took his title from Vimy and retained the name in 1928 when he was created viscount. In 1921 Byng came to Canada and assumed his duties with a high respect for Canadians, gained from his intimate wartime associations. He set out to explore the country from coast to coast and visited far into the North, including a trip down the Mackenzie River and along the Arctic ocean coastline.

In 1926, he found himself the central figure in an explosive constitutional issue. Prime Minister Mackenzie King, carrying on in the House with the aid of the Progressive party, faced a vote of censure and feared defeat. He asked Byng to dissolve Parliament so that a general election could be held. Byng refused and asked Arthur Meighen, Conservative opposition leader to form a government. Meighen tried but was quickly defeated in the House. King held that Byng should follow the advice of the Sovereign's Canadian Prime Minister. He was returned to power, the constitutional issue was clarified and thereafter, Governors General were bound to abide by the recommendations of the Canadian government.

Byng returned to England in 1926 and in 1928 was appointed Commissioner of the Metropolitan Police in London, He relinquished the post in 1931. He died in 1935.

Lord Willingdon

(1926-1931)

A seasoned diplomat, as well as a cultured and widely-travelled nobleman, Freeman Freeman-Thomas, Baron Willingdon of Ratton and Earl and Marquess of Willingdon, was the thirteenth Governor General.

Born September 12, 1866, he was educated at Eton and Trinity College, Cambridge. He went to Australia in 1897, where he served for three years as aide-de-camp to his father-in-law, Lord Brassey, Governor of Victoria, then returned to enter the House of Commons. He remained there until he was elevated to the peerage and joined the House of Lords in 1910, when he was also appointed Lord-in-Waiting to King George V.

In 1913, he was named Governor of Bombay; in 1919, Governor of Madras; and in 1926, prior to his Canadian appointment, he chaired a mission to China on the Boxer Rebellion indemnities. He took his oath of office in Quebec City on October 2, 1926.

Willingdon visited many parts of the Dominion and made goodwill visits to the United States. He was warmly received everywhere he went. Early in his tenure, the Statute of Westminster was signed and the Governor General became the sole representative of the Crown in Canada, taking his advice from the Sovereign's Canadian advisors. The British government then appointed a British High Commissioner to Ottawa to act as liaison between the government of Canada and the United Kingdom. Canada had previously established a High Commissioner's office in London.

In 1927, he entertained the Prince of Wales on his historic tour of Canada, and the British Prime Minister, Ramsay MacDonald. He also set a precedent by flying from Ottawa to Montreal, the first Governor General to take to the air.

On completion of his term of office in 1931, he went directly to India as Viceroy, a post that had been held by three of his predecessors. He later carried out many important missions for his country; he was raised to the rank of marquis and made Chancellor of the Order of St. Michael and St. George. He died in London in 1941.

Lord Bessborough

(1931-1935)

The 9th Earl of Bessborough, a soldier, politician and businessman, became Canada's fourteenth Governor General.

Born Vere Brabazon Ponsonby, October 27, 1880, he received his education at Harrow and Trinity College, Cambridge. Though trained for the legal profession and a member of the bar, he chose politics as a career at twenty-six, but suffered a number of defeats. He sat in the House of Commons for a total of approximately seven years, then went to the House of Lords in 1920, when he succeeded to the earldom on the death of his father. He fought at Gallipoli and in France and after the war became a wealthy and powerful figure in the business world.

Appointed to the vice-regal post in 1931, like many of his predecessors, he was sworn in at Halifax. For the first time, the swearing-in ceremony was broadcast over a Canadian and United States radio network.

Lady Bessborough, née Roberte de Neuflize, was a member of a wealthy, titled French banking family. A beautiful woman, she was a welcome chatelaine in a country with some three million French-speaking people.

The Bessboroughs' hobby was amateur theatrics and they had frequently written and presented shows in the theatre of their English home. In Canada, they fostered the organization of the Dominion Drama Festival which has had a continuing influence on the Canadian stage.

Lord Bessborough's tenure covered the worst part of the world economic depression, and he insisted on sharing in the general reduction of salaries in the public service. The Bessboroughs travelled widely throughout Canada and talked intimately with all classes and all ages.

Lord and Lady Bessborough returned to England late in 1935, taking with them a son, George St. Lawrence Neuflize, born a few months after their arrival in Canada. Bessborough re-entered the business world and had interests in many countries, but still carried out important public services.

He died in Hampshire, England, on March 10, 1956.

Lord Tweedsmuir

(1935-1940)

A highly successful novelist and historian, John Buchan was the first of his profession to become Governor General of Canada. A man of many talents, he was also a lawyer, a diplomat, a war correspondent, a publisher and a member of the House of Commons for the Scottish Universities seat.

Born in Perth, Scotland, August 26, 1875, the son of a clergyman, Buchan enjoyed a distinguished academic career. But he was first and foremost a writer and prior to coming to Canada, he had earned an enviable reputation as an author. He is known for such mystery novels as *The Dancing Floor* and *The Thirty-Nine Steps.*

On his appointment as Governor General in 1935, he became Baron Tweedsmuir, taking his name from the ancestral home in Scotland, the scene of many happy boyhood memories.

While in office, he travelled widely and frequently across Canada and undertook the longest single trip of any Governor General to date, 19 000 kilometres across Canada, down the Mackenzie River to the Arctic Circle and deep into isolated communities along the North Pacific coast of British Columbia.

In 1936 he was made honourary president of the Canadian Authors' Association and he instituted the annual Governor General's awards for Canadian literature. Though many of his predecessors had visited American presidents informally, in 1937 Lord Tweedsmuir paid the first state visit to the White House. He was guest of the Roosevelts and addressed the U.S. Senate. Poor health forced him to undergo medical treatment in England from August to October 1938, following which he resumed his vice-regal duties. In 1939 he entertained King George VI and Queen Elizabeth during their historic tour of Canada and the United States.

His term of office was to expire in November 1940, but he died in February in a Montreal hospital while undergoing surgery for a head injury sustained in a fall. He was accorded a state funeral in Ottawa and his ashes were returned to his homeland.

The Earl of Athlone

(1940 - 1946)

The Earl of Athlone, Canada's sixteenth Governor General, was the second member of the royal family to occupy the vice-regal post.

Born on April 14, 1874, Alexander Augustus Frederick William Alfred George Cambridge was the third son of the Duke of Teck and Her Royal Highness Princess Mary, daughter of the Duke of Cambridge.

Educated at Eton and the Military College at Sandhurst, Athlone made soldiering his career. He won distinction and high honours in the Matebeleland African campaign; in the South African War and the First World War.

Named Governor General of Canada in 1914, he refused the post because of the outbreak of war. In 1923, he was made Governor General of South Africa and served until 1930, a total of seven years, and later became Governor and Constable of Windsor Castle. He was reappointed to Canada and took office on June 21, 1940.

With the world in the throes of the Second World War, many of his early activities were in connection with Canada's war effort, which he supported with a wisdom born of wide experience and a constant optimism in the outcome of the struggle.

Like his predecessors, Athlone studied Canada intimately through constant travel. He visited President Roosevelt at Hyde Park in 1940; and again in 1945, he and the countess, Princess Alice, the last surviving granddaughter of Queen Victoria, were guests of the White House at a state dinner. They were probably the last distinguished visitors to meet President Roosevelt, who died a few days later of a stroke.

Momentous events were crowded into Athlone's tenure, mostly associated with the war and the comings and going of leaders, including the two Churchill-Roosevelt war conferences held in the Citadel in Quebec, the summer residence of the Governor General.

Athlone ended his term in March 1946 and returned to England. He died in London on January 16, 1957.

Lord Alexander

(1946-1952)

The seventeenth Governor General, the last titled holder of the office, and probably the most universally popular of all before him, was Viscount Alexander of Tunis, who was Field Marshal and Deputy Commander to General Eisenhower in the last stages of the Second World War.

Born on December 10, 1891, Harold Alexander was the third son of the 4th Earl of Caledon in County Armagh, Ireland, and was educated at Sandhurst for an army career. Before he was twenty-eight, he had commanded a battalion of Irish Guards on the western front in the First World War and won the Military Cross, the Distinguished Service Order and Legion of Honour.

In 1939, at the outbreak of the Second World War, Alexander commanded the first division in France. As Commander of the First Army Corps, he directed the stand at Dunkirk and the evacuation, and was the last man to leave the beach. In 1942, he directed the difficult and tragic withdrawal from Burma. When India was threatened he was made commander of the forces in the Middle East. He was leader in the most important campaigns in North Africa, Sicily, Italy, the Balkans and finally at the surrender in southwest Europe.

Alexander, his lovely wife Margaret, daughter of the Earl of Lucan, and their three children came to Ottawa on April 12, 1946, when he was sworn in at a great ceremonial in the Senate chamber.

Alexander mixed with Canadians to an unprecedented degree. He skied, skated, square-danced, made maple sugar, painted and was an ardent sports fan. He travelled widely and was a familiar figure all over the Dominion and in Washington. He entertained Princess Elizabeth, the Duke of Edinburgh and Prime Minister Churchill. He also witnessed the end of the Mackenzie King era; Canada's longest-serving Prime Minister retired in 1948 and died in 1952.

By popular request, his term was extended twice, but early in 1952 he was recalled to England for the important post of Minister of Defence which he held until 1954.

Business interests occupied him after his term in the government, interests which frequently brought him to Canada where he had a host of friends and admirers. He died in Windsor, England, June 16, 1969.

Vincent Massey

(1952-1959)

When Prime Minister St. Laurent needed a successor to Lord Alexander as Governor General, he decided on the choice of a Canadian for the post. He selected a brilliant son of a rich Canadian manufacturing family, the Right Honourable Vincent Massey, who was born in Toronto February 20, 1887. His nomination received swift royal assent and soon gained general approval from the Canadian public.

Vincent Massey was no stranger to public service. He was educated at the University of Toronto, and at Oxford, and lectured for a time at the University of Toronto. His brother, Raymond Massey, was a leading actor of stage and screen.

He was Canadian Minister to Washington for four years and was High Commissioner in London from 1935 to 1946. Throughout the war years, he and his wife played hosts to thousands of Canadian service personnel. He was appointed to the U.K. Privy Council in 1941 and was made Companion of Honour in 1946.

In 1949-51 he headed the Royal Commission on National Development in the Arts, Letters and Sciences which produced a monumental and authoritative report on Canadian cultural development. He was an optimistic and dedicated worker in the cause of national unity.

Conscious of his role as Canada's first Canadian Governor General, Mr. Massey travelled widely to meet Canadians from all walks of life and even flew over the North Pole on a special flight. He is the author of many works, including a collection of his speeches and an autobiography. On one occasion, as guest of honour at the annual dinner of the Parliamentary Press Gallery, his address was in the form of a witty narrative poem, which has since become a collector's item.

Mrs. Massey died in 1950 and the chatelaine at Rideau Hall during Massey's tenure was his daughter-in-law, Mrs. Lionel Massey. There were many formal functions and each winter a program of informal dances for young people.

His term of office exceeded seven years and in 1959 he retired to his home, Batterwood House near Port Hope, Ontario, where he died in 1967.

General Georges-P. Vanier

(1959-1967)

General Georges-Philias Vanier was seventy-one years old when he became nineteenth Governor General, the second Canadian to hold office. He brought to it a distinguished record of service to his country in war and peace.

Born in Montreal on April 23, 1888, he studied law and was admitted to the bar in 1911. But from 1915 until his death, war and public service occupied the greater part of his life. He was commanding officer of the Royal 22nd Regiment from 1925 to 1928.

He earned decorations and distinction during the First World War. Thereafter he represented his country on numerous diplomatic missions and at important conferences dealing with postwar problems and adjustments.

General Vanier served as Secretary of the Canadian High Commission in London and was Canadian Minister to France when that country fell in 1940. He returned there as Canadian ambassador from 1944 until his retirement in 1953 at the age of sixty-five.

Despite this retirement, he was frequently engaged in government missions, including delegations to the United Nations, and in private business activities. Honours and decorations were showered on him as they had been throughout most of his active life, both at home and abroad.

General Vanier was no stranger to Rideau Hall, having served as aide-de-camp to Governors General Byng and Willingdon. A tall, impressive man with great dignity and composure, he moved about with some difficulty due to the loss of a leg in the First World War, but the impairment never hindered the enthusiasm and dedication with which he carried out the duties entrusted to him. On his appointment as Governor General in 1959, he set out at once to emulate his predecessors in getting to know Canada and its people. In his first year of office, he travelled some 25 000 kilometres. He worked hard and incessantly for the cause of national unity and to encourage a greater awareness among Canadians of the value and importance of happy, united family units.

A soldier to the end, he valiantly fought ill-health in an effort to discharge the numerous centennial responsibilities of his office, but succumbed on March 5, 1967, the second Governor General to die in office.

Following a state funeral in Ottawa and a memorial service in Quebec's historic Citadel, General Vanier was buried in Quebec City with full military honours.

Roland Michener

(1967-1974)

Although he had been a Conservative parliamentarian and a Conservative party choice for Speaker of the House of Commons, there was little surprise when Rt. Honourable Roland Michener became a Liberal appointee for the post of High Commissioner in India. It was even less surprising when he was nominated by a Liberal government as the twentieth Governor General, the third native Canadian to occupy the position.

Appointed after the sudden death of the able and much-loved General Vanier, Michener returned from New Delhi and took office April 17, 1967, in time to plunge into the arduous though pleasant task of welcoming the almost daily arrivals of heads or high representatives of state making centennial year visits to Canada.

Assisted by his wife, herself an author, musician and doctor of philosophy, the new Governor stepped gracefully and easily into his new role. Genial, imperturbable, full of political wisdom and world knowledge, he possessed an even, temperate understanding that carried him through the Speakership in two stormy parliaments, including one in which no party had an absolute majority.

A handsome, urbane, silver-haired combination of lawyer-businessman-politicodiplomat, Daniel Roland Michener was born April 19, 1900 at Lacombe, Alberta, the son of a senator. He was educated at the University of Alberta and is a Rhodes scholar from that institution. He completed his legal training at Oxford, was admitted as a barrister of the Middle Temple in 1923, and opened a practice in Toronto. His education was interrupted briefly when in his eighteenth year he entered the Royal Air Force.

Michener represented a Toronto riding in the legislature from 1945 to 1948, part of which time he was Provincial Secretary. He was elected to the House of Commons in 1953 and again in 1957, when he was elected Speaker, a post he held until the general election of 1962, when he was defeated.

He was appointed to New Delhi in 1964, and was studying Hindi at the time he was recalled to Canada. He also mastered French years earlier to help him in his parliamentary career.

After serving as Governor General, he returned to his law practice with Lang, Michener, a legal firm he helped establish in 1927. He died August 6, 1991 and his ashes rest at St. Bartholomew's Church, Rockliffe Park.

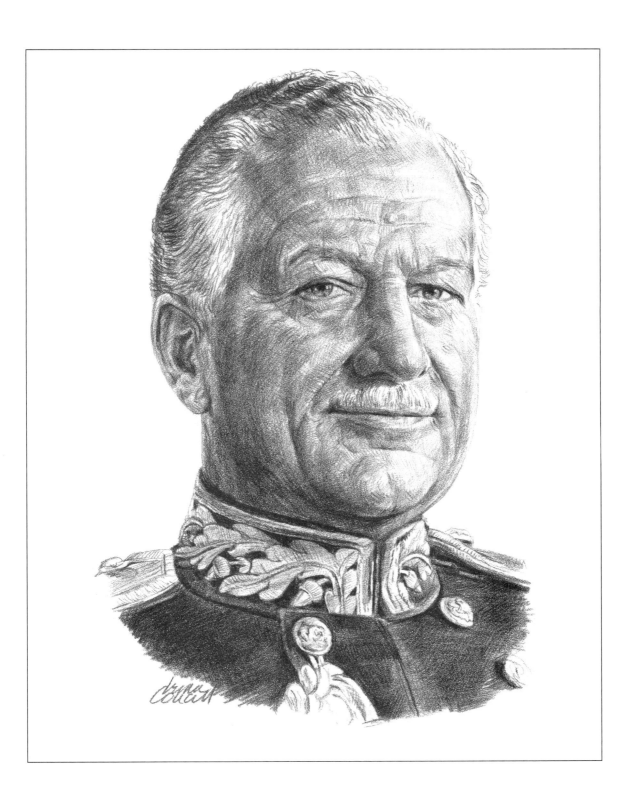

Jules Léger

(1974-1979)

Jules Léger was born April 14, 1913 in the village of St. Anicet, Quebec, where the St. Lawrence widens to become Lac St. Francois.

As a boy, helping in the family store for 10 cents a week, Jules gained an early understanding of the Christian warmth of family life and the friendship and mutual dependence of a small village.

Jules Léger attended Valleyfield College and studied law at the University of Montreal. He obtained his doctorate at the Sorbonne in Paris in 1938.

On his return to Canada he became associate editor of the Ottawa daily *Le Droit* for a short time. In 1940 he joined the department of External Affairs and was seconded to the office of Prime Minister Mackenzie King, who at that time was also Secretary of State for External Affairs. This was the beginning of a brilliant diplomatic career. Léger has served as Canadian ambassador in many world capitals, including Mexico City, Rome, Brussels and Paris. He was Under-Secretary of State for External Affairs from 1954 to 1958, when he was appointed Canada's representative to the Organization for European Economic Co-operation and permanent Canadian representative to the North Atlantic Council from 1958 to 1964. In November 1968 he assumed the position of Under- Secretary of State, with responsibilities in the fields of arts and culture, bilingualism, education and citizenship.

Léger was appointed Governor General on January 14, 1974. He retained his personal touch but with a determination to see that the Governor General should play a useful, even significant, part in the life of the nation. Léger believed his office should enrich the average Canadian's knowledge of his country and his fellow Canadians. Greatly aided by Madame Léger, he sought to encourage governments at all levels and the citizens themselves to develop a deeper sense of national identity and to be more aware of this country's unique good fortune.

In June 1974 Léger suffered a stroke which impaired his speech and left a partial paralysis of the left arm. But, thanks to will-power and determination, by the summer of 1978 his health seemed much restored. Those with him enjoyed once more the quick humour and insight of his mind.

Jules Léger's life of devotion and service ended November 22, 1980. The mourning at the State Funeral at the Basilica in Ottawa and at the service and burial in Valleyfield, Quebec, was eased by gratitude for his spirit and the quality of his life.

Irma
Coucill

Edward Schreyer

(1979-1984)

First elected to the Manitoba Legislative Assembly at the age of twenty-two, Edward Richard Schreyer went on to become Premier of his province and, later, the twenty-second Governor General of Canada.

Born at Beausejour, Manitoba, on December 21, 1935, to John and Elizabeth Schreyer, he is a descendant of pioneer farmers. He studied in Winnipeg at United College, St. John's College and the University of Manitoba, where he earned the degrees of Bachelor of Arts, Bachelor of Education, and Master of Arts in International Relations and Economics. During this time he served as second lieutenant in the Canadian Officer Training Corps, Royal Canadian Armoured Corps. In June 1960, he married Lily, daughter of Jacob Schulz, former M.P. for Springfield, Manitoba.

After his election to the Legislative Assembly in 1958, he was returned in 1959 and 1962. In 1965 he made the leap to federal politics, winning the Springfield seat in the general election. He was re-elected as M.P. for Selkirk in 1968.

Schreyer resigned his seat in the House of Commons when he was chosen leader of the Manitoba New Democratic Party in June 1969. His bid for a return to provincial politics was realized later that month when he was elected M.L.A. for Rossmere, and became Premier of Manitoba. In 1977 his party was defeated, and he became Leader of the Opposition.

Schreyer's appointment as Governor General on January 23, 1979 came as a surprise to many people, including Schreyer himself. At forty-two, he was much younger and less well known than most previous Governors General. Since his appointment, he has turned his attention to national energy policy and the problems of Canadian unity.

The Governor General travelled widely throughout Canada, including the North, and he undertook a heavy programme of engagements, involving thousands of persons from all walks of life, at his residences in Ottawa and Quebec. Their Excellencies also paid State visits to Norway, Sweden, Denmark, and Iceland in June 1981. For these occasions, the Schreyer Fellowships were established to enable Scandinavian researchers to visit Canada. The first award of the Schreyer Cup for Soccer was made, and organization meetings were held for the Governor General's Study Conference.

Following his term as Governor General, Schreyer was appointed Canada's high commissioner to Australia in 1984. He returned to Canada as a private citizen in February 1988. Now living outside Winnipeg, he is a visiting lecturer on political issues at several universities.

Irma Coucill

Jeanne Sauvé

(1984-1990)

The twenty-third Governor General of Canada was born Jeanne Benoît in Prud'homme, Saskatchewan on April 26, 1922. She was educated at Notre Dame du Rosaire convent in Ottawa and studied at the University of Ottawa. She married Maurice Sauvé on September 24, 1948 and then moved with her husband to Europe, studying in London and Paris where she obtained a diploma in French Civilization from Université de Paris.

Returning to Canada in 1952, Mrs. Sauvé began a twenty year career as a freelance journalist and broadcaster. During this time she had one child and was active in organizations such as the Union des Artistes, YMCA, Bushnell Communications, the Institute of Political Research and the Canadian Institute of Public Affairs.

Entering politics in 1972, and appointed Minister of State for Science and Technology Mrs, Sauvé became the first female Member of Parliament from Quebec to become a Cabinet Minister. She later became Minister of the Environment and Minister of Communications and was known as an able administrator, capable of providing decisive leadership and dealing with complex concepts.

On April 14, 1980, Mrs. Sauvé was elected the first woman Speaker of the House of Commons. She completely overhauled the administrative and financial operations of the House of Commons, streamlining personnel, increasing efficiency and services and saving $18 million. She also opened the first daycare centre on Parliament Hill before her Speakership ended on November 30, 1983.

Mrs Sauvé was appointed the 23rd Governor General and the first woman Governor General of Canada on December 23, 1983 and was installed on May 14, 1984. The main themes of her mandate were peace, national unity and concern for young people, and she travelled extensively throughout Canada to bring the viceregal office to the people.

Before returning to a private life on January 29, 1990, Mrs. Sauvé established a $10 million youth foundation which bears her name. She died in Montréal, Quebec on January 26, 1993.

Ramon John Hnatyshyn

(1990-1995)

Canada's twenty-fourth Governor General was born the grandson of Ukrainian immigrants in Saskatchewan on March 16, 1934. He grew up and attended university in Saskatchewan, receiving his Bachelor of Arts in 1954 and his Bachelor of Laws in 1956 from the University of Saskatchewan.

Upon graduation he was admitted to the Bar of Saskatchewan in 1957. Hnatyshyn also began serving as a member of the Royal Canadian Air Force 23rd Wing Auxiliary in 1956, before going to Ottawa as the executive assistant to the leader of the government in the Senate in 1958. In 1960, Hnatyshyn returned to his home province to practice and teach Law.

In 1974, Hnatyshyn was elected to the House of Commons as a Progressive Conservative . Over the course of his political career, he held a number of cabinet positions which included Minister of State for Science and Technology (1979), Minister of Energy Mines and Resources (1979-1980) and Minister responsible for Regulatory Affairs (1986). In 1986, Hnatyshyn was admitted to the Bar of Ontario and appointed to the position of Minister of Justice and Attorney General of Canada where he served until 1988.

In 1988, he was appointed Queen's Council for Canada. In 1989 he was awarded the St. Volodymyr Medal Award from the World Congress of Ukrainians for his contributions to justice and civil liberties.

On January 29, 1990, Hnatyshyn became Governor General. At the beginning of his mandate, Hnatyshyn identified four personal themes, which he consistently supported: the environment, literacy, seniors and voluntarism. He established the Governor General's Performing Arts Awards in 1992, the Fight for Freedom Literacy Award and the Environmental Engineering and Environmental Science Scholarships.

Hnatyshyn brought dignity and warmth to the Governor General's office and reopened the 88 acre Governor General's estate to the public. Rideau Hall, the only one of Canada's seven official residences open to the public has become a fortunate amalgam of living museum and art gallery as well as retaining it's position as Canada's national meeting place for heads of state, diplomats and Canadians from across the country.

Roméo LeBlanc

(1995-   )

Born in Memramcook, New Brunswick on December 18, 1927, Roméo LeBlanc became the first Governor General of Acadian heritage. He was also the first Atlantic Canadian, the first former Senator and the first former member of the Press Gallery to hold the position.

At l'Université St-Joseph, Memramcook, LeBlanc earned a Bachelor of Arts in 1948 and a Bachelor of Education in 1951. He then spent a brief period as a teacher, before taking time away in 1953 to study French Civilization at l'Université de Paris.

In 1960, LeBlanc turned to journalism, working as a correspondent for Radio-Canada in Ottawa until 1962. He was a correspondent in the United Kingdom from 1962 to 1965 and then in the United States from 1965 until 1967. This experience led to LeBlanc serving as Press Secretary to Prime Ministers Lester B. Pearson and Pierre Elliott Trudeau. In 1972, LeBlanc was elected to the House of Commons to represent the riding of Westmorland-Kent in New Brunswick. He was a cabinet minister from 1974 to 1979 and 1980 to 1984.

As Canada's longest serving fisheries minister, LeBlanc won a lasting reputation as a friend of the fishermen. He helped to develop Canada's 200 mile fishing limit and to shape the International Law of the Sea. His leadership promoted conservation and resource management which in turn encouraged strong growth in the fishing industry during the late 1970s and early 1980s.

In 1984, LeBlanc became a Senator and was appointed Speaker of the Senate in 1993.

On February 8, 1995, LeBlanc became the twenty-fifth Governor General of Canada. One of the first and recurring concerns that LeBlanc has kept close to his heart is Canada's propensity for generosity, acceptance and compassion. He credits these characteristics in part to Canada's unique heritage, and expresses a strong belief in the importance of studying and teaching Canadian history. The Governor General's Caring Canadian Award, which he launched in 1995 acknowledges the everyday courage and dedication of ordinary people who, every day, make extraordinary contributions to their families, community or country.

In his installation speech, LeBlanc remarked that if he were to be known for anything he would hope it would be for encouraging Canadians, knowing a little bit about their extraordinary daily courage, and for wanting that courage to be recognized. He also expressed a strong belief that Canada's greatness as a country comes from its citizens.

Irma Coucill

Fathers of Confederation

The Fathers of Confederation were the thirty-six statesmen who took part in one or all of the conferences in Charlottetown, Quebec and London from 1864 to 1867, when the resolutions forming the basis for federal union were adopted. These resolutions were written into the British North America Act, proclaimed July 1, 1867, creating the Dominion of Canada—Ontario, Quebec, New Brunswick and Nova Scotia—with its capital in Ottawa.

These were not the founders of Canada—there had been a Canada for well over two hundred years—but they were the founders of the Canada of today. They were dreamers and visionaries, but time transformed their dreams and visions into reality. They surveyed this land of unlimited space and resources, realized its potential and knew what must be done to take advantage of the priceless heritage.

Confederation was not a sudden thing, nor the product of a revolution. It was a peaceful evolution that had been simmering a score or more years before the historic Charlottetown Conference of September 1864.

At that time there was a desperate need for transportation and communication between the communities of British North America; and a desperate need for political stability, economic betterment and amity between French and English peoples. Those who saw these needs, grappled with them and worked out a formula to meet them were mostly native Canadians. Only ten of the thirty-six founders were born outside the country—four in England, two in Scotland, two in Ireland, one in Bermuda and one in New York.

But all were Canadians when they started their campaign for confederation, and all had experience as members of some branch of a legislature or federal parliament. There were twenty lawyers in the group as well as six editor-publishers and writers.

In their lifetimes, ten Founders were to be provincial lieutenant-governors, nine provincial premiers; sixteen were members of the post-confederation House of Commons and twelve were federal cabinet ministers. Twelve were in the Senate and eight became high court judges. Thirteen of the Founders were awarded knighthoods. Two died at the hands of assassins.

Those were strenuous days and living involved what the civilization of today would consider unbearable hardships. Survival itself was difficult and medical services and sanitation were primitive. The Fathers lived lustily and worked hard according to the records. They ate well and many drank freely. Yet they were a healthy generation; many lived to their 70s; twelve lived well into their 80s and three lived into their 90s.

Confederation came when it did because of the actions of John A. Macdonald, Liberal leader George Brown and French Canada's leader, George-Etienne Cartier. In 1864, apparently at the willingness of Brown to enter an agreement with the other parties, these three men combined to form the Great Coalition and pledged, among other things, to bring about some sort of federal union and break the existing political stalemate. Also, through union, they proposed to create transportation facilities and develop the economic potential of the country.

Having helped to launch the final surge toward confederation, Brown dropped out of the political picture, preferring to play his part in the building of Canada through the editorial columns of his newspaper, the Toronto *Globe*.

Adams George Archibald

Adams George Archibald was born May 18, 1814 in Nova Scotia's central town, Truro. He received his higher education in the Academy at Pictou and studied law in Prince Edward Island. He returned to the mainland and practised law near his birthplace.

He became involved in the struggle for responsible government. In 1851 he won election as a Liberal in his home county of Colchester. After five years' experience, he became Solicitor General and, four years later, Attorney General. (His second interest was education; he advocated a free system for the whole province.) When Joseph Howe retired after his defeat in 1863 by the young Dr. Charles Tupper, Archibald took his place as leader of the opposition.

Tupper had agreed to the uniting of the Maritime Provinces, as a first step in a wider union, and arranged that the three provinces should send five delegates each to Charlottetown to discuss the possibilities. As leader of the opposition, Archibald was invited to be a delegate and continued a staunch confederationist through the ensuing conferences at Quebec and London, and entered Macdonald's first administration as Secretary of State.

In 1870, after McDougall's unfortunate experience with the Riel Rebellion, Archibald was named Lieutenant-Governor of Manitoba and for three years laboured to lay sure foundations of government in the new province.

He returned to Nova Scotia and succeeded his old leader, Joseph Howe, as Lieutenant-Governor, from 1873 to 1883. He resumed his interest in educational matters, first as chairman of the board of governors of Dalhousie College in Halifax and then as president of the Nova Scotia Historical Society. But politics was in his blood; he was re-elected to the House of Commons and represented his old constituency of Colchester for three years, from 1888 to 1891. He died December 14, 1892.

George Brown

George Brown, son of an Edinburgh merchant, was born 65 kilometres up the Forth at Alloa, November 29,1818. He grew up and was educated in the Scottish capital.

When twenty years of age, he migrated with his father, first to New York and then to Toronto, where he founded the *Globe* as a weekly newspaper in 1844 and as a daily in 1853.

Brown was a man of deep convictions. He opposed state support to all denominational schools. He advocated representation by population, to give the large population of Canada West its due weight in the assembly. He argued for the annexation of the Hudson's Bay Company's lands. He reorganized the Reform party. For a brief two days in 1858 he held power as Premier of the province.

Sectionalism had become so firmly rooted in both provinces that Parliament floundered; governments changed almost yearly. To break this deadlock, many considered a larger union essential. It was at this point, in 1864, that Brown rose to his full stature as a statesman. One day he stood up, walked forward to meet Macdonald, and offered his support in bringing about confederation. The incident reveals the personal sacrifice Brown was prepared to make for his adopted homeland.

He worked faithfully at the conferences, but found his connection with Macdonald irksome. When he fell out with Galt on the reciprocity question in 1865, he resigned. He still supported confederation but believed the Conservatives should form the government and the Liberals the opposition. But Macdonald took many of the ablest Liberals into his cabinet and so weakened Brown's leadership that Brown was personally defeated in the 1867 elections.

Though Brown was made a senator in 1873, he confined his efforts mainly to the columns of his powerful newspaper. He died on May 9, 1880, from a bullet wound inflicted by a disgruntled employee.

Sir Alexander Campbell

Alexander Campbell was born in Yorkshire, England, March 9, 1822. When he was a year old, he was brought to Canada by his doctor father. He was educated at St. Hyacinthe in Quebec and at the grammar school in Kingston, Ontario. He studied law and shortly after being called to the bar, became a partner of John A. Macdonald. The partnership grew into a close and enduring friendship.

At the early age of thirty-six, Campbell was elected to the legislative council of the united Canadas. (In 1857 election to the council had become an alternative to appointment.) In 1864 he was made Commissioner of Crown Lands and went as a delegate to the conferences at Charlottetown and Quebec. On the achievement of confederation, he was given a seat in the Senate, became Conservative leader there and entered the cabinet as Postmaster General. In 1873, shortly before the fall of the government, he was moved to the Department of the Interior. He continued his leadership in the Senate; when the party was returned to power in 1878, he was knighted and occupied, in turn, the offices of Receiver General, Postmaster General, Militia and Defence, Justice and again Postmaster General. In 1887 he became Lieutenant-Governor of Ontario and with Sandford Fleming represented Canada that year at the first colonial conference.

Campbell proved himself a man of unquestioned integrity. Macdonald looked upon his old friend as an experienced administrator to whom he might safely assign any task. Campbell repaid the trust with wise and impartial advice on appointments. Nor did he hesitate to criticize the government. A note to Macdonald in 1885 reads, ' ... the country is impoverished by expenditure which is unnecessary and fruitless.'

He died May 24, 1892, near the close of his five-year term as Lieutenant-Governor.

Sir Frederick Carter

Frederick Bowker T. Carter was a home-grown Newfoundlander, born in St. John's, February 12, 1819, educated in her schools, and admitted to her courts in 1842.

He became a member of the legislature, representing various constituencies in turn: Trinity, 1855-1865, Burin, 1865-1873, and Twillingate, 1873-1878. From 1861 to 1864, he was Speaker of the House and led the Newfoundland delegation to the Quebec Conference, taking with him the leader of the Liberals, Ambrose Shea. At the conference, he was won over to the idea of confederation. He became Premier in 1865 but, in spite of his personal popularity, his party suffered defeat on the confederation issue in the election of 1869. Carter was again Premier from 1874 to 1878.

Special tasks assigned to him are clear evidence of the esteem in which he was held by his fellow citizens. When, on different occasions, the colonial economy broke down, Carter was given wide administrative powers by the imperial government to pull the colony out of its difficulties. He played a large role also in fisheries disputes with other countries. On surrendering Newfoundland in 1713, France had retained certain fishermen's rights on the west coast and on part of the north coast for the purpose of drying their codfish and mending their nets. This arrangement greatly hampered Newfoundland fishermen. Worse still, the French government gave a bounty to their fishermen that enabled them to undersell the colonists on the world market. There was trouble too with aggressive American fishermen. Carter accepted leadership in negotiating a settlement of these disputes and was highly regarded for his efforts on behalf of the people.

In 1878 he was knighted for his services. In the following year he was appointed to the Supreme Court of Newfoundland and in the next year became Chief Justice. He died March 1, 1900.

Sir George-Etienne Cartier

George-Etienne Cartier, son of a soldier, was born September 6, 1814 in St. Antoine, Lower Canada. He was educated in Montreal and opened a law office there in 1835. Two years later, his youthful daring and profound dislike for arbitrary government led him into the camp of rebellion with Louis-Joseph Papineau.

Entering politics, he represented Verchères from 1848 to 1861 and Montreal East from 1861 to 1872. He became a staunch supporter, loyal colleague and close friend of Macdonald in several administrations and leader in one of them.

Living at the centre of Canadian business activity in Montreal and moving in the same circles as Alexander Galt, he became greatly interested in trade and in railway building. He felt that his French compatriots should plunge into these commercial fields on equal footing with the English. He supported the building of the Grand Trunk Railway, acted as that company's solicitor, and diligently promoted the Canadian Pacific Railway. In his view, these enterprises carried great commercial possibilities for his province.

Confederation held no terrors for Cartier. He believed that French Canada could protect its distinctive culture better in a federation than in the existing union of the Canadas. Together with the mutual trust of Macdonald and Cartier, the confidence reposed in Cartier by the French Canadians was one of the most vital factors in the achievement of confederation. He was a delegate at all the conferences. In the first federal parliament, he was made Minister of Militia and Defence — a far cry from his position thirty years back!

In the summer of 1870, during Macdonald's four-month illness, Cartier took over the leadership of the government. In 1872, in the hope of regaining his own failing health, Cartier sailed for England, but he died in London, May 20, 1873.

Edward Barron Chandler

Chandler's parents came to Nova Scotia in the loyalist migrations and settled in Amherst, on that strip of land connecting Nova Scotia and New Brunswick. Here Edward was born August 22, 1800. Here he went to school, studied law and was called to the bar in 1823. Shortly thereafter he moved into New Brunswick.

He was elected to the legislative assembly for the County of Westmorland and held the seat from 1827 to 1836. For the years 1844 to 1858, he served on the executive council. He was a delegate to the conferences and gave general support to confederation, but expressed strong dislike for the extensive powers being given to the central government. He was offered a seat in the Senate but declined, choosing to remain in the provincial field.

He shared the eagerness of his fellow Nova Scotian, Joseph Howe, to see a railway built to connect the Maritime Provinces with the St. Lawrence colonies, 'passing wholly through British territory.' He accompanied Howe to Canada in 1851 and together they secured an agreement to build an intercolonial railway. This agreement was ratified by their respective governments. When guaranteed loans for the project could not be obtained, Nova Scotia and New Brunswick turned to the building of railways within their own borders.

In 1862 the idea of an intercolonial railway was revived and in 1864 its construction became a condition of the Maritime Provinces' consent to enter confederation. Work was started in 1867, and, because of his interest in the project from the beginning, Chandler was made commissioner in charge of construction. The road was completed in 1876 and Chandler saw his dream fulfilled.

In 1878 Chandler succeeded Sir Leonard Tilley as Lieutenant-Governor of New Brunswick. He died two years later in Fredericton, February 6, 1880.

Jean-Charles Chapais

Jean-Charles Chapais was born in Rivière Ouelle, December 2, 1811, and was educated in the Quebec Seminary. His father was a prominent merchant and when Jean-Charles grew up he joined his father and continued in the business for twenty years. It was this experience that he brought to bear, later, on the business of government.

He entered Parliament as Conservative member for Kamouraska from 1851 to 1867. He was given the portfolio of Public Works in the Great Coalition of June 1864. He was present at Quebec, along with the whole Canadian cabinet, which included the other French-Canadian ministers, George-Etienne Cartier · and Hector Langevin.

When confederation came into being, Chapais was sitting as member for Champlain County. He continued in the new provincial assembly and at the same time was appointed to the Senate in the federal field. In those days, it was permissible to hold office in both provincial and federal legislatures.

From his seat in the Senate, he directed the Department of Agriculture (1867-1869) and the Ministry of Receiver General (1869-1873). When the Conservative party lost control in 1873 over the Canadian Pacific scandal, Chapais was able to carry on in the Senate. He was not included in Macdonald's reconstructed cabinet of 1878.

Chapais died July 17, 1885.

James Cockburn

Like several other Fathers of Confederation, James Cockburn came from the British Isles. He was born at Berwick, England, February 13, 1819.

James was thirteen when his family migrated to Canada. They settled in Toronto and James received his education in the recently founded Upper Canada College. He was a full-fledged lawyer at twenty-seven and set up his practice in the lakeside town of Cobourg, one of the most progressive centres in the province.

In 1861 he was elected to the legislative assembly by his home county, Northumberland. After three years' experience in Parliament, he became Solicitor General, and like all other coalition ministers, became a delegate to the conference at Quebec.

The delegates from the Maritime Provinces were taken on an extended tour of the Canadas, as far west as Niagara. Like other junior ministers, Cockburn had not much to say at Quebec. But Cobourg was one of the points on the tour and Cockburn made it the occasion for a pleasant supper meeting for the delegates, their wives and daughters.

When the federal Parliament was organized, Cockburn was chosen unanimously to be the first Speaker of the House of Commons. In a Parliament where opinions were so sharply divided, this was no small chore. For seven years Cockburn, a man of courtesy, tact and firmness, set a high standard for the important office of Speaker of the House.

He died in Ottawa, August 14, 1883.

George Coles

George Coles was born in Prince Edward Island, September 20, 1810. He learned the management of the family brewing and distilling business, to which he later became heir.

In 1842 he was elected to the provincial assembly from Queen's County and held the seat for twenty-six years. He played the principal part in the successful struggle for responsible government of the Island. He was also a determined opponent of the absentee landlords who still owned much of the land on the Island.

Coles and his Reform colleagues had been in favour of a general union of the British North American provinces but they disliked the scheme drawn up at Quebec because it gave too much power to the federal government and because it made no provision for buying out the absentee proprietors.

The provincial assembly, in 1865, almost unanimously signified that no inducements could make them change their minds. And the general election of 1867 returned Coles and the Reform party to power.

However, by 1873, the Island found itself in financial difficulty, due chiefly to the overbuilding of railways, and was prepared to enter the Dominion on the basis of new proposals.

In the meantime, a breakdown in mental health, partly due to the destruction of his properties by fire, had forced Coles' retirement in 1868. He died August 21, 1875.

Robert Barry Dickey

Robert Dickey was born in Amherst, Nova Scotia, November 10, 1811, eleven years after his fellow-townsman and confederation colleague, Edward Chandler, and ten years before another fellow-townsman and colleague, Charles Tupper. He was educated at Windsor Academy and began his law practice in 1834. Chandler had moved out of Amherst, but three years later another 'father,' Jonathan McCully, moved in. The young Dr. Tupper returned from Edinburgh University and set up his medical practice there in 1846 and became a close friend of Dickey. The town of Amherst had quite a bit to do with confederation!

Dickey was not particularly interested in the hurly-burly of political life, but accepted readily an appointment to the legislative council, possibly on the suggestion of his good friend, Tupper, who had become Provincial Secretary.

When in 1864 Maritime union was being considered, Dickey was picked by Tupper as the Conservative delegate to Charlottetown and later to Quebec. McCully was the Liberal representative. Dickey was the most outspoken Nova Scotian critic of the Quebec plan. He agreed with Coles of Prince Edward Island and Chandler of New Brunswick that too much power was given to the federal government. He was in favour of the general principle of union and supported Tupper's resolution for a final conference in London.

When the federal elections were held, Dickey did not seek a seat in the House of Commons, but accepted an appointment to the Senate. A somewhat reluctant politician, he took a decreasing part in public affairs. He was rated a wealthy man and an influential citizen and possibly considered law his real career.

He died July 14, 1903, in his ninety-second year.

Charles Fisher

Charles Fisher was a citizen of Fredericton, New Brunswick, from his birth on August 15, 1808 till his death on December 8, 1880. His father was a loyalist historian and was interested in a good education for his son. Charles was a member of the first graduating class of King's College, Fredericton, the present University of New Brunswick. He finished his studies in 1833.

He was elected to the New Brunswick legislature in 1837 and came forward as a strong champion of responsible government, at a time when such views were frowned upon by upper-class citizens. He was no polished orator; 'awkward and uncouth in speech and manner but probably the coolest head and best brain of the lot.' He was a member of a committee charged with the task of getting the provincial laws arranged in good order.

New Brunswick was plagued with frequent changes of government; the issues confronting the province included responsible government, prohibition of liquor and confederation. Fisher became Premier in 1854 as the leader of the vigorous Reform party, called the 'Smashers,' and held the portfolio of Attorney General. As the result of some political indiscretion, he resigned in 1861.

He was a delegate to Quebec. Though he lost his seat in the general election of 1865, he regained it in the highly significant York by-election six months later. Tilley and fellow confederates won the crucial election of the next year. Fisher, as Attorney General, went to London to assist in framing the British North America Act.

He was elected to the federal House in 1867 from his old constituency of York and had the honour of moving the adoption of the Speech from the Throne in the first session. In the following year, he resigned his seat to become a member of the Supreme Court of New Brunswick—a position for which he was well prepared.

Sir Alexander Tilloch Galt

Alexander Tilloch Galt was born in London, England, September 6, 1817 and came to Canada in 1835 when his father, the novelist John Galt, became commissioner of the Canada Land Company with responsibility for the land settlement of the Huron Tract between Lake Erie and Lake Huron. Alexander himself became a clerk with a similar land company in the Eastern Townships of Quebec, where he was soon promoted to be commissioner of the company.

Shortly after, he entered Parliament as independent member for Sherbrooke. Politician and businessman, he used his contacts to further the commercial interests of Canada and of his land company by arranging for the building of the Montreal-Sherbrooke-Portland railway, giving Montreal a winter port.

In 1858 Galt became Minister of Finance in the Cartier-Macdonald administration of the united Canadas on condition that the long-talked-of confederation of the British North American provinces (including the North-West) should be a firm plank in the government's platform. Confederation was made a practical issue with the backing of Cartier and Macdonald.

At Quebec, it was Galt who worked out the plan to have the federal government take over all provincial debts on a basis of equality, making confederation financially workable.

When the government was formed in 1867, Galt became Minister of Finance —a field in which he was universally trusted. Following disagreements, he left the cabinet. In 1872 he dropped out of politics and devoted his time to such matters as the Atlantic fisheries and his private enterprises in Western Canada.

In 1880 Macdonald made him the first High Commissioner for Canada in London. Galt was characteristically enthusiastic but undiplomatic and returned to Canada three years later.

He died in Montreal, September 19,1893.

John Hamilton Gray

(Prince Edward Island)

There were two Fathers of Confederation bearing precisely the same name, John Hamilton Gray. This one was born in Prince Edward Island in 1812. He was educated at Charlottetown and, embarking on a military career, served as a cavalry officer in India and South Africa.

Returning to his native province, he entered politics in 1858 as a member for Queen's County. In 1863 he was re-elected and became Premier.

Proposals for a union of the Maritime Provinces had little appeal for the Islanders: there was small prospect that Charlottetown would become the capital of the proposed union; they would lose their provincial legislature and their existence as a province. Moreover, they wanted no part in the railway debts being accumulated in the other two Maritime provinces. Gray himself had little interest in a local union. Charles Tupper probably had these attitudes in mind in choosing Charlottetown as the proper place for the conference.

The introduction of the idea of a wider union had scarcely more appeal for the people, but considerably more for Gray, Pope and other leaders. The Charlottetown Conference was a bit embarrassing for the host premier, presiding at a meeting that was distasteful to so many of the citizens. No careful arrangements had been made for the accommodation of the delegates; the hotels were filled by crowds of people in town to attend a circus. There was no welcoming committee; the members of Parliament, too, may have been at the show!

Gray, now definitely interested in the broader union, went on to Quebec. The Island delegates did not speak with one voice; some of them were quite opposed. On his return to the Island, Gray found himself in the minority in his own cabinet. He got into a public row with his colleague Palmer and resigned.

He retired from politics and went back to military affairs as head of the militia. He died near Charlottetown, August 13, 1887.

John Hamilton Gray

(New Brunswick)

This John Hamilton Gray was born in 1814 in Bermuda, where his father was the British consul for Bermuda and Virginia. When the family moved to Nova Scotia, young Gray won his degree at King's College, Windsor, and studied law in Saint John, New Brunswick.

He entered the legislature from St. John County as a Liberal in 1851, but within a year turned Conservative. In the next ten years he held various offices: Attorney General, Premier, Speaker of the House.

Outside the House, he acted as chairman of a Nova Scotia commission on the question of state aid to a church institution-his old King's College. Later, he was named by the imperial parliament as chairman of a Prince Edward Island commission to settle the land disputes between proprietors and tenants.

Gray was a man of honour, with a fine legal mind. It was he who pointed out the legal contrast between the former American colonies and the present British provinces; the colonies were sovereign states, the provinces were not. In consequence, a different formula was found for the division of fields of legislation as between central and provincial parliaments in the new Dominion.

Gray steadily and strongly supported Tilley in the explanation and defence of the Quebec Resolutions. He was elected for Saint John in 1867 and was made chairman of the Committee of Supply. The post was not burdensome and gave him leisure to record the events of confederation as he remembered them. He finished the first volume of this history in 1872. In that same year he left parliamentary life to become a judge in the Supreme Court of British Columbia. For some reason, possibly remoteness from the scene of the events, the second volume, that was to have brought the story up to the admission of British Columbia, remained unfinished at the time of his death, in Victoria, June 5, 1889.

Thomas Heath Haviland

Thomas Heath Haviland, born in Charlottetown, November 13, 1822, was brought up in a political atmosphere; his father had been in politics longer than the son could remember. Young Haviland received his elementary education in Charlottetown and his higher education in Brussels. He was articled in law and was called to the bar in 1846.

At the very early age of twenty-five, he became a member of the legislative assembly and acted, in turn, as Colonial Secretary, Speaker of the House and Solicitor General. In 1870, he was appointed to the legislative council and again acted as Colonial Secretary.

Haviland was not at the Charlottetown meeting, but he and Whelan were the two additional representatives in the larger delegation sent to Quebec. In their group of five, Palmer steadily became anti-confederate, but Haviland, Gray, Pope and Whelan became enthusiastic supporters of confederation and stoutly defended it in public.

But the people were not ready for confederation; they preferred to go it alone. When harder times came and debts piled up, they were ready to listen to new proposals from Canada. Haviland was one of three commissioners who succeeded in arranging the better terms that brought the Island into the confederation fold in 1873.

Following this, Haviland was given a seat in the Canadian Senate. Six years later he resigned to become Lieutenant-Governor of the island province.

He died in Charlottetown, September 11, 1895.

William Alexander Henry

William Alexander Henry was a lifelong Haligonian. He was born in Halifax, December 30, 1816; received his education locally; studied law and started his law practice in 1840, and died there May 3, 1888.

At twenty-five years of age, with the support of the great Joseph Howe, he was elected as Liberal member for Antigonish, a largely Roman Catholic constituency, though he was a Protestant. But in 1857, Howe, commissioner in charge of railway construction, denounced the violence of Roman Catholic workers on the right-of-way and thereby alienated Catholic support for the party. Henry resigned his position as Provincial Secretary and went over to the Conservative party.

In the Tupper administration of 1863, Henry became Attorney General and an obvious choice as one of the delegates to the conferences. He was not particularly active at Quebec, but in London he registered his fear that the appointed Senate might thwart the will of the elected Commons and suggested that the government of the day should be given authority to create new senators to override determined opposition. A clause was inserted in the British North America Act permitting the appointment of three or six (now four or eight) additional senators on the recommendation of the Governor General. This measure of course lessens in some degree that independence for which the Senate was created.

Defeated in the election of 1867, Henry returned to his law practice in Halifax. In 1875 he was appointed to the Supreme Court of Canada where he served till his death.

Sir William Pearce Howland

William Howland was born at Paulings, New York, May 29, 1811. He came to Upper Canada and set up in business at Cooksville in 1830. In 1840 he bought the Lambton Mills on the Humber River and later entered the wholesale groceries business in Toronto.

He was interested in the Reform movement but kept clear of Mackenzie's extreme views. He took out citizenship papers in 1841 and linked his future with the promising young country.

In 1857 he was elected on a Reform platform to the legislative assembly of the Canadas and served in various coalition cabinets: Minister of Finance 1862, Receiver General 1863, Postmaster General 1864 and Finance Minister again in 1866.

He was a delegate to the final London Conference, taking the place of Mowat who had been appointed to the bench in Canada West. Like Henry, he had a suggestion for curbing the blocking-power of the Senate: have them appointed for a fixed term by the provinces!

Howland and George Brown disagreed regarding future relations with coalition, from which Brown had already resigned. The matter came up for debate at the Reform convention in Toronto. Brown was determined that they should return to party politics. Howland argued that eastern Reformers like Tilley would be in the federal cabinet, that Liberals in Canada West had been asked not to desert their comrades, and that he himself would continue to cooperate with Macdonald. Led by Brown, the convention decided to leave the coalition and withdrew party support from Howland and McDougall.

In spite of the lack of official party support, Howland was elected, was created a C.B. and was made Minister of Inland Revenue. However, he felt his position as spokesman for the party greatly weakened and retired at the close of the first session.

From 1868 to 1873 he was Lieutenant Governor of Ontario. As he was still only sixty-two, he resumed his business interests in Toronto. He died in his ninety-sixth year, January 1, 1907.

John Mercer Johnson

Johnson was another among the Fathers of Confederation who was of British birth; he was born in Liverpool in October 1818. As a boy he was brought to New Brunswick and received his education at the Northumberland grammar school. In 1840 he became a fully licensed lawyer.

In 1850 he became the Liberal member for his county and when his party came to power under Fisher in 1854 his name appeared in the list of cabinet ministers along with those of Tilley, Ritchie, Steeves and others—the 'Smashers' administration.

In the following years Johnson had wide experience in the various departments of provincial government: Solicitor General, Postmaster General, Speaker of the House and Attorney General. There was no surprise at his being chosen as a delegate to all three conferences.

Like Chandler, Johnson, though a confederationist, took exception to one feature of the Quebec Resolutions: the great strength given to the central government. There was wide variety of opinion regarding the relative importance of the provincial and federal parliaments; probably the arrangement made represents a fair compromise.

Like all other assembly delegates to Quebec, Johnson lost his seat in the election of 1865, but he regained it the next year and in the following year won a seat in the federal house. His experience in that field was regrettably brief; he died November 9, 1868.

Sir Hector-Louis Langevin

Hector-Louis Langevin was born in Quebec City, August 25, 1826. His father was a soldier and a strict disciplinarian. Hector attended the seminary in Quebec, studied law under the businesslike Cartier and opened his own office in 1850.

In 1857 he was elected to the Canadian assembly for Dorchester. In succession, he was Solicitor General and Postmaster General under the kindly eye of his old mentor, Cartier. And as did Cartier, Langevin displayed wholehearted trust in Macdonald's loyalty to the French-speaking people. Quite naturally, he was one of the Lower Canada delegates to the confederation conferences.

In 1867 he was elected for his old constituency, was awarded a C.B. and named Secretary of State. Two years later he moved over to the office of Public Works. When Cartier died in 1873 the mantle of French leadership in the government fell upon Langevin. Later that year the Conservatives lost power because of the railway scandal.

When a Conservative come-back was made in 1878, Langevin became Postmaster General and later returned to the office of Public Works. He was given a knighthood in 1881.

Ten years later investigation uncovered extensive corruption in Langevin's department. Langevin's personal record was clear, but being responsible for the department, he resigned from the cabinet. In that same year Macdonald died. It fell to Langevin, senior member of the party, to make the announcement to Parliament. In the course of his tribute to his late chief, Langevin was overcome with emotion and could not continue. As the leader of the opposition, young Wilfrid Laurier, remarked, Langevin's silence was more eloquent than any words he could have spoken.

Langevin died in Quebec City, July 11, 1906.

Andrew Archibald Macdonald

Macdonald's family had migrated directly from Scotland in 1806. Andrew was born in Three Rivers, Prince Edward Island, February 14, 1829. After a grammar school education, strengthened by private tutoring, he went into business as a merchant and shipowner. This was the era of the sailing ship and the fleets of the Maritime Provinces ranked high in the world of commerce.

Macdonald became a member of the legislative assembly in 1853, for a five-year term. In 1863 he was elected to the legislative council, and in the following year was sent to Charlottetown and Quebec, the youngest of the 'fathers.' His personal notes on the conferences were published in the March 1920 number of the *Canadian Historical Review.*

Like other members of the Prince Edward Island delegation at Quebec, Macdonald was a vigorous critic of the federal plan proposed by the Canadians. He objected particularly to the distribution of the seats in the Senate and argued strongly in favour of a larger representation of senators from the Maritime Provinces.

When Prince Edward Island backed away from confederation in 1867, Macdonald stayed on in the legislative council and shortly became a member of the executive council or cabinet. When the Island came into union in 1873, Macdonald joined the federal civil service as postmaster at Charlottetown.

In 1884 he became Lieutenant-Governor of his native province for a five-year term. Later he was appointed to the Senate, where he served until his death, in Ottawa, March 21, 1912.

Sir John Alexander Macdonald

John Alexander Macdonald was born of Highland parents in Glasgow, January 11, 1815. The family migrated to Kingston, Upper Canada in 1820. The father's limited success in various ventures took the family to Hay Bay, to Glenora and finally back to Kingston. Throughout, the mother insisted upon the lad's schooling. He was a lawyer at the age of twenty-one.

He lived in the midst of stirring events: political discontent, rebellion, union of the Canadas with Kingston as one of the capitals. He had his first political experience in 1843, as an alderman. The next year he was elected to Parliament by a large majority.

Conservative fortunes were at a low ebb. Macdonald sought to rebuild them along liberal-conservative lines: responsible government, commercial development, honest co-operation with Lower Canada. In these endeavours he was markedly successful.

But his greatest achievement was confederation itself. He was able to enlist the aid of men of diverse opinions and to guide wisely their deliberations, whether as Premier of the Canadas, as leader of the Canadian delegation at Quebec, or as chairman of the London conference.

In the selection of a federal cabinet in the face of so many competing claims, Macdonald had need of all his statecraft. It may have been with a touch of pardonable pride that, on a later visit to Province House, Charlottetown, he signed the visitors book "John A. Macdonald, cabinet builder.' Without Macdonald, possibly there could have been no confederation at that time.

Confederation from sea to sea went forward through the five-year term of the new Parliament and its work was approved in the election of 1872. Then followed defeat in 1873 and recovery five years later.

In 1884, on the fortieth anniversary of his entrance into parliamentary life, he was given a G.C.B. The following year he was privileged to see the completion of the Canadian Pacific Railway. He died June 6, 1891.

Jonathan McCully

Jonathan McCully was born in Cumberland County, Nova Scotia, in July 1809. As so many young persons without money have done, McCully went into teaching as a stepping-stone to further education. (One bright lad in his classes was Charlie Tupper.) McCully later studied law, was called to the bar and opened an office in Amherst—a town that seems to have a considerable concentration of Fathers of Confederation. Chandler was born there in 1800, Dickey in 1811 and Tupper in 1821.

In 1848 McCully was appointed a member of the legislative council and moved to Halifax to be near his work. He served consecutively as Solicitor General, Commissioner of Railways, government leader. For eight years he acted as editor of the *Morning Chronicle*, the most important newspaper in the Maritime Provinces.

When Tupper was picking the delegates for Charlottetown he invited the leader of the opposition in the assembly, Archibald, and asked him to name a Liberal team-mate. Archibald chose McCully, who was at the time leader of the opposition in the legislative council.

McCully came back from Quebec more enthusiastic than ever for confederation and advocated the cause in his editorials. Suddenly, the tone of the editorials was reversed; McCully had been dismissed by the paper's anticonfederate proprietor, William Annand, who was then publishing Howe's 'Botheration Scheme' letters as editorials. McCully became editor of the *Morning Journal*, renamed by him the *Unionist*.

The versatile teacher-lawyer-editor-politician was able to render good service in the three conferences and was awarded a place in the Senate in 1867. In 1870, he left the Senate to become a judge in the Supreme Court of Nova Scotia, where he served till his death on January 2, 1877.

William McDougall

William McDougall was born near Toronto, January 25, 1822. He attended local schools and graduated from Victoria College, then in Cobourg. He became a lawyer, a member of the 'Clear Grits' and founder of that party's paper, the *North American*. When this paper was absorbed by the *Globe* McDougall became closely associated with George Brown.

Elected to the assembly of the united Canadas, he was made Commissioner of Crown Lands and later provincial Secretary. Unlike Brown, McDougall did not leave the coalition in 1865 and this marked the parting of the ways for the two men. He argued, 'We think that the work of the coalition is not done but only begun ... I think the coalition ought not to cease until the work, begun under Mr. Brown's auspices, is ended.'

In the first parliament after union McDougall presented a resolution favouring the cession of Hudson's Bay Company lands to Canada. He and George-Etienne Cartier went to England and arranged for this transfer to take place December 1, 1869. In the fall of 1869 McDougall, named Lieutenant-Governor of Rupert's Land, proceeded to the Red River country via the United States.

A very mixed population had developed in the Red River area: descendants of the Selkirk settlers, retired servants of the Hudson's Bay Company, migrants from Canada, newcomers from the United States and, outnumbering all these, a closely-knit group of Métis farmers, hunters and trappers, stoutly opposed to any change. On this latter group, McDougall's announcement of the new ownership fell like a thunderbolt. The Métis, under Louis Riel, took up arms and blocked McDougall's entry. Frustrated, he returned to the east and resigned.

Through Donald Smith, chief commissioner of the Hudson's Bay Company, Macdonald began negotiations with the Red River Settlement and these ended in Manitoba's admission to the union as a province in 1870.

McDougall lived on for many years, re-entered political life but was never so prominent again. He died May 29, 1905.

Thomas D'Arcy McGee

D'Arcy McGee was born at Carlingford, Ireland, midway between Belfast and Dublin, April 13, 1825. In 1842 widespread hardship drove him with many others to America. He had an Irishman's inclination to talk and to write, and he did both well. He went into journalism. In a few years he returned and worked on various Irish newspapers, until his connection with the 1848 rebellion forced him to flee to New York, where he again took up writing. In 1857 he was induced by Irish Roman Catholics to come to Montreal to found the *New Era*.

From journalism he moved easily into politics, representing Montreal West, and found himself working with George Brown. Personal antagonism drove them apart and McGee became a Conservative. He loyally supported the British connection and denounced Fenian extremists, thereby incurring their lasting hatred.

McGee was one of the first public persons to see clearly the danger that might threaten Canada at the conclusion of the American Civil War. He toured the British provinces, fanning, with his passionate oratory, the fires of patriotism for a great new nation, the only alternative to disaster. Similar appeals appeared in his writings—historical, political and poetical.

His efforts entitled him to a place in the first federal cabinet, but, recognizing Macdonald's problems in meeting regional, ethnic and religious demands, McGee, with Tupper, stood aside. Macdonald sent an appreciative note to McGee: 'The difficulties of adjusting representation in the cabinet from the several provinces were great and embarrassing. Your disinterested and patriotic conduct—and I speak of Tupper as well as yourself—had certainly the effect of removing those difficulties.'

Macdonald planned to make McGee Commissioner of Patents and so provide him with leisure for literary work. This was all cut short in the early hours of April 7, 1868, when McGee, returning from a late session, was shot down at his own door by a young Fenian sympathizer, Patrick James Whelan.

Peter Mitchell

Peter Mitchell was very much a New Brunswicker. He was born January 14, 1824 at Newcastle, went to its grammar school, read law and in 1848 set up a practice there. He later left the profession and was engaged in two of New Brunswick's characteristic industries —lumbering and shipbuilding.

In 1856 he entered the provincial assembly as an independent from Northumberland and in 1861 was appointed to legislative council. For five years he was a minister in the Fisher and Tilley administrations. He attended the Quebec Conference and strongly supported union. In the 1865 election the confederationists were defeated badly. Next to Tilley, Mitchell was the man who reversed the verdict in 1866.

As a businessman, he was able to meet the objections of Saint John bankers who feared the loss of business to the Canadas. He also won the support of lumbermen, fishermen, and shippers of the 'north shore' by his insistence that the proposed intercolonial railway should follow the Gulf of St. Lawrence and not the inland route. As Tilley was not back in Parliament, Mitchell, a member of the legislative council, was asked to form a government with R.D. Wilmot as joint premier. Tilley became Provincial Secretary. With four other New Brunswick delegates, Mitchell went to London to negotiate his province's entrance into confederation.

In 1867 he was appointed to the Senate and acted as Minister of Marine and Fisheries for five years. But his independence of mind led him to resign his office and to seek a seat in the House of Commons. At this time also he became editor and afterwards owner of the Montreal *Herald*.

During the last three years of his life he acted as Inspector of Fisheries for the Maritime Provinces. He died October 25, 1899.

Sir Oliver Mowat

Oliver Mowat was born at Kingston, July 22, 1820. From his Scottish Presbyterian parents he inherited firmly held religious convictions; he considered Christian statesmanship his vocation. He attended private schools and studied law in the office of his fellow townsman, John A. Macdonald, and was called to the bar in 1841.

In 1857 he became Liberal member for Ontario South in the assembly of the Canadas and served first as Provincial Secretary and then as Postmaster General. Somewhat reluctantly, Brown, Mowat and McDougall entered the Great Coalition on the promise that the constitutional issue would be settled. They would have preferred giving the support from outside the government.

As a cabinet minister, Mowat was a delegate to the Quebec Conference, where he was responsible for the resolution concerning the legislative powers of the provincial governments. Soon after the conference he resigned to become vice-chancellor of Upper Canada. On the resignation of Edward Blake in 1872, Mowat became Premier of Ontario for the next twenty-four years. Acting also as Attorney General, he introduced voting by ballot in provincial and municipal elections and extended the franchise.

Mowat was not one of the chief architects of confederation but he did much to determine the form taken by confederation in its first forty years. When he became responsible for Ontario affairs, he waged many battles for provincial rights and won most of them. In this way, Mowat was responsible, possibly more than any other, for the power acquired by the provincial legislatures to act as fully responsible bodies in matters of provincial concern.

With Laurier's coming to power in 1896, Mowat, who had been made a K.C.M.G. four years before, was appointed to the Senate as government leader and Minister of justice. He found the work too demanding for a man of seventy-seven and retired within a year. He was given the G.C.M.G. and named Lieutenant-Governor of Ontario. He died in Toronto six years later, April 19, 1903.

Edward Palmer

Edward Palmer was born in Charlottetown, September 1, 1809. He received his general education in the local schools and his legal education in his father's office. His own son became a third-generation lawyer by the same route.

Palmer spent thirty-eight years in parliamentary work; twenty-five of them as representative of Queen's County, 1835 to 1860, and thirteen as a member of the legislative council, 1860 to 1873. During these years he occupied many offices: Solicitor General, Attorney General, President of the Council and further terms as Attorney General.

He attended the Charlottetown and Quebec conferences but, along with George Coles and A.A. Macdonald, Palmer was one of the most determined opponents of the Quebec Resolutions. Realizing that little could be done to improve the Island's representation in the House of Commons, 5 in 194, Palmer felt frustrated and resentful. He spoke of himself as the 'malcontent of the conference.'

At times he seemed prepared to drop his opposition, as when, in Toronto, he said the Island delegates 'will not hesitate to recommend to the people the great union which I hope shortly to see adopted.' But home once more, he came out squarely against union. He continued his opposition until 1873 when he and Macdonald reversed their stand and accepted the 'better terms' offered by Canada.

At this time Palmer left political life, became a county court judge for a year, and for fifteen years Chief Justice of the Supreme Court of his province. He died in office, November 4, 1889.

William Henry Pope

William Henry Pope was born at Bedeque, Prince Edward Island, May 29, 1825. He was sent to England for his education, but returned to Charlottetown where he studied law in the office of Edward Palmer. He was called to the bar in 1847.

In 1859 he had the unusual experience of being named Colonial Secretary, though not a member of the legislature; the government was trying the experiment of having civil servants head the government departments. When he became the representative for the constituency of Belfast, on the south shore, in 1863, he was continued in that office. As a minister in Gray's Conservative administration he was one of the hosts to the delegates in 1864. The elaborate luncheon given by him in his own spacious house and grounds on the outskirts of Charlottetown set the congenial tone of the gathering.

Pope was an early convert to the idea of British American union and gave vigorous support to the Quebec Resolutions in his newspaper *The Islander*. And when the government rejected confederation outright in 1866, he resigned his office in protest. He then prepared a careful article, 'The Confederation Question from the Prince Edward Island Point of View,' setting forth a reasoned statement of just what union would mean for the gulf province. He never wavered in his devotion to the dream and lived to see its fulfillment.

With the entry of his province into confederation in 1873 Pope resigned his seat and became judge of Prince County.

He died in Summerside, October 7, 1879. His place in history has been obscured somewhat by the name of his better-known son, Sir Joseph Pope, the close associate and literary executor of Sir John A. Macdonald.

John William Ritchie

John William Ritchie was born in Annapolis, Nova Scotia, March 26, 1808. He was brought up in a legal atmosphere; his father was the county judge. He was educated privately and became a qualified lawyer at twenty-five.

His first public office was as law clerk to the legislative council in Halifax. He later became a member of the council and was then taken into the cabinet as Solicitor General.

He maintained a steady support of confederation, particularly for commercial advantages expected to follow. He felt that the renewal of the Reciprocity Treaty with the United States should be the concern of all the provinces and not of the Canadas only. He acted on the Confederate Council on Commercial Treaties which met at Quebec in the autumn of 1865 to study the whole question of colonial trade. In their resolutions the council boldly suggested: that the provinces should take joint action in commercial policies, that trade missions be sent to the West Indies and to South America, and that one of their members be invited to act with the British minister in the Washington negotiations.

His work on this committee brought him into greater prominence and, partly as a result of this, he was named as a delegate to the final conference in London.

In 1867 he was appointed to the Senate and three years later to the Supreme Court of Nova Scotia.

In 1873 Ritchie was made a judge in equity in which office he served for nine years. In this period, sharing with Archibald an interest in such matters, he too became president of the Nova Scotia Historical Society.

He died in Halifax, December 18, 1890.

Sir Ambrose Shea

Ambrose Shea was born in St. John's, Newfoundland, September 17, 1815. His father was one of the well-to-do merchants who largely controlled the affairs of the island. Ambrose grew up in the family business.

In 1848 he was elected as Liberal representative of Placentia and held a seat in the assembly for nearly forty years. In 1855 he became Speaker of the House and later Colonial Secretary. He was leader of the opposition when he was invited to the conference at Quebec.

Shea was an active delegate, especially concerned with the poverty of his countrymen, for which he hoped confederation would prove a helpful and readily acceptable prescription. But he had not taken account of the newness of the idea to Newfoundlanders and their easily aroused fears of losing their legislative independence. And he did not anticipate the opposition of his own merchant class, with their power to influence their fishermen clients. Merchants were doing quite nicely with things as they were and spoke to their customers of increased taxes, higher prices, and other dreadful economic consequences of confederation.

In the general election, the Carter-Shea coalition government feared to make confederation an issue, and the project was quietly dropped; Newfoundland's joining had to be written off for the near future at least.

Shea's services to the colony itself were recognized in the granting of a K.C.M.G. in 1886 and in a nomination to the governorship of the island. However, this appointment was so widely opposed by the colonists that Shea was moved to the governorship of the Bahamas, where he served from 1887 to 1895.

He died in London, England, July 30, 1905.

William Henry Steeves

William Henry Steeves was born at Hillsborough, on the Petitcodiac River in New Brunswick, May 20, 1814. His family were lumbermen and shipbuilders and young William grew up in the Steeves Brothers business. He and Mitchell would be able to understand each other.

In 1846 he became Liberal member in the legislative assembly for Albert County and held the seat for a five-year term. He was then appointed to the legislative council and named a member of the executive, first as Surveyor General for a year and then as Minister of Public Works for eight years.

Railways were very much in the minds of the people of New Brunswick at this time, and Steeves was in the centre of the movement. He was one of several men who were interested in an intercolonial railroad, quite apart from confederation. Steeves, with other Maritimers, met with Canadians in Quebec in 1862 to discuss the matter and the related question of free trade among the provinces. Probably because of this businessman's approach to problems, Steeves was named as one of New Brunswick's delegates to the conferences at Charlottetown and Quebec.

He did not take an outstanding part in the discussions but gave the union movement his steady support. Being a member of the legislative council, he did not lose his seat as did all the New Brunswick delegates who were members of the assembly.

On the completion of confederation, Steeves was chosen as a representative of New Brunswick in the Senate, along with Peter Mitchell.

He died at Saint John, December 9, 1873.

Sir Etienne-Paschal Taché

Etienne Taché was born September 5, 1795, at St. Thomas de Montmagny. His family was descended from the explorer, Louis Jolliet. He took his schooling in the seminary at Quebec and, while still in his teens, enlisted in the militia and fought in the War of 1812. He then studied medicine and set up practice in his home town, where he was looked up to as a dignified country gentleman.

From 1841 to 1846 he represented L'Islet in the legislative assembly of the united Canadas. From 1846 to 1848, with the rank of colonel, he was in charge of the Lower Canada militia. Appointed to the legislative council, he was made a member of the Baldwin-Lafontaine administration, acting in turn as Commissioner of Public Works, Receiver General and Speaker of the House. In a debate in 1846, he delivered his famous declaration of French-Canadian loyalty to the British crown: ' ... we will never forget our allegiance till the last cannon which is shot on this continent in defence of Great Britain is fired by the hand of a French Canadian.'

In 1856 he became first minister of the Taché-Macdonald administration, but usually deferred to Macdonald as the leader from the legislative assembly. Because of ill-health, he resigned after only one year in office. For his services he was knighted shortly afterwards and made an honorary colonel of the British Army and aide-de-camp to Queen Victoria.

In 1864, because of his impartiality and high-mindedness, he was called out of retirement to give leadership in the desperate political situation prevailing. As the first minister of the host province, Taché was chosen to preside at the meetings of the Quebec Conference.

Taché's death on July 30, 1865 necessitated a new coalition. As Brown could not bring himself to serve under either Macdonald or Cartier, a less prominent leader was chosen, Sir Narcisse Belleau.

Sir Samuel Leonard Tilley

Samuel Leonard Tilley was born of loyalist parentage at Gagetown, New Brunswick, May 8, 1818. He received some education at the local grammar school but left when he was thirteen for the big city, Saint John, and worked for seven years in a drug store. He joined the Young Men's Debating Society and developed his natural ability in public speaking. At twenty, he acquired his own very profitable medical supply business.

He got into politics without trying; his backers took the matter in hand. He became Provincial Secretary and as a teetotaler and prohibitionist had a prohibition act passed that might have wrecked his career. From this experience he learned to respect public feeling and did much useful work in railway building, political reform, and education.

As Premier and Provincial Secretary, he was chief delegate to the conferences on confederation —a proposal inherently distasteful to many people in New Brunswick. With the term of Parliament ending in 1865, Tilley considered it fatal to try to push through the scheme in the last few months of the session; so he agreed to put the question to the electors. The anti-confederates won three to one; all three assembly delegates to the conferences, Tilley, Gray and Fisher, were defeated; the union seemed a lost cause.

In 1866 external pressures and internal divisions brought a distinct reversal in favour of union and Tilley was returned to power. New Brunswick joined Nova Scotia in asking for another conference—a final one in London.

In the new Canada, Tilley was Minister of Customs and then Minister of Finance, but resigned in 1873 to become Lieutenant-Governor of New Brunswick. He re-entered Parliament in 1878, and as Minister of Finance, introduced the National Policy in the budget speech of 1879, and received a knighthood.

In 1885, because of failing health, he left active political life and became Lieutenant-Governor again. In broken health, he retired in 1893 and died in Saint John, June 25, 1896. His great strength lay in the courage with which he held his course, facing confidently the storm of shorter-sighted opposition.

Sir Charles Tupper

The original Tuppers came from England to Connecticut in 1635. A century later, Charles' grandfather moved to Nova Scotia. Charles was born July 2, 1821 at Amherst, the birthplace also of Chandler and Dickey. He was educated at Wolfeville, went to the University of Edinburgh for his degree in medicine and took up practice in his native town in 1843.

In 1855 young Dr. Tupper had the audacity to run against the able, experienced and popular leader of the Reform party, Joseph Howe—and beat him. He was given the portfolio of Provincial Secretary. His purposeful energy carried him to the premiership when Johnson, the Premier, was made a judge in 1863. He proposed a legislative union of the Maritime Provinces a few weeks before Brown presented his resolution on the federal union of the British American provinces. He was chief delegate for Nova Scotia at all the conferences.

The people of Nova Scotia did not take kindly to the Quebec scheme. Howe and other anti-confederates filled their minds with fears of the unknown: direct taxes, beggarly subsidies, outside interference and loss of the British connection. The tide was strong against union.

Tupper knew that he dared not submit the scheme for legislative approval. He stalled for time, even dragged in the dead issue of union in the Maritimes. In due course the tide turned; the possibility of American attack, the threat of Fenian raids, the cancellation of the Reciprocity Treaty were all factors in convincing most men that some kind of union was a necessity.

In the first Canadian Parliament, Tupper suggested that he and McGee should solve Macdonald's problems regarding the cabinet by stepping aside. He later occupied various offices: Inland Revenue, Customs, Public Works, Railways and Canals.

In 1883 he was appointed High Commissioner of Canada in London and, with the exception of a year as Minister of Finance, occupied that post till 1896. He then became Secretary of State in the Canadian House of Commons for three months and Prime Minister until the government was defeated in June. For four years he led the opposition and then retired.

His patriotism, courage and patience enititled him to a place of high honour. He was knighted in 1879 and made a baronet in 1888. Last of the 'fathers,' he died in Kent, England, October 30, 1915.

Edward Whelan

Edward Whelan was born of Roman Catholic parents in Mayo County in western Ireland in 1824, and was brought with the family to Halifax at twelve years of age. While still a lad he entered the employ of Joseph Howe to learn the printing trade. Howe must have seen some promise in his young apprentice; he advised him to read widely and to practice public speaking. On his own part, Whelan must have had a fair share of ambition; at nineteen, with Howe's encouragement, he moved to Charlottetown, Prince Edward Island, and started a Reform newspaper of his own, *The Palladium*.

In his paper he attacked the absentee property owners, charging them with vicious greediness. He received wide support in every way but financially. His followers were the people without much money. His paper went bankrupt and he was reduced to accepting the editorship of his hated rival, *The Morning News*.

At twenty-two years of age, he was elected to the provincial legislature from King's County. In a fresh venture a year later, he founded *The Examiner* and used its columns to join the fight being waged by George Coles for responsible government. He was so outspoken that he found himself frequently being sued for libel. The victory was finally won in 1851.

In that year of good fortune he entered the executive council or cabinet and also became the Queen's Printer, a natural appointment.

He was a delegate to the Quebec Conference and sent home to his paper lively accounts of the discussions, the parties and the tours. In 1865 he published the story of the two conferences, *The Union of the British Provinces*.

He held King's County until 1867, and remained a strong supporter of confederation to the end. He was disappointed and dismayed when the electors who had sustained him for twenty years turned against him. He died December 10 of the same year.

Robert Duncan Wilmot

Robert Wilmot, a member of a prominent New Brunswick family, was born in Fredericton on October 16, 1809. He was educated in Saint John and went into the lumbering and shipping business, as did Steeves and Mitchell later.

In 1840 he became interested in liberal ideas and was elected to the legislature in 1846. Not a confirmed party man, he accepted office in the Conservative cabinet as Surveyor General in 1851 and as Provincial Secretary in 1856.

Wilmot became an anti-confederate after studying the Quebec Resolutions. Many New Brunswick anti-confederates were pretty well unionist at heart, but opposed the Quebec scheme because, as Albert J. Smith and others held, it gave too much power to the central government, or, as Wilmot and others contended, it left government too weak.

These strange bedfellows, Smith and Wilmot, headed the anti-confederate government formed after the overthrow of the Tilley administration in 1865. As might be expected, it proved to be a very contentious and ineffective administration.

Wilmot was a member of the Confederate Council on Commercial Treaties, embracing all the provinces. From his observations while attending a meeting of the council at Quebec, he became convinced that Canada East would never accept legislative union; if there was to be a union at all, it would have to be a federal union as planned at Quebec.

Wilmot resigned from the Smith-Wilmot administration in March 1866, and with Mitchell formed a confederate government when Smith resigned one month later. He also became a new member among the confederation delegates to the London meeting.

In the formation of the government of Canada, Wilmot was given a seat in the Senate. In 1878 he became Speaker of the Senate and Minister Without Portfolio in Macdonald's reconstructed administration.

In 1880 he resigned his seat in the Senate to become Lieutenant-Governor of his home province. He died February 12, 1891.

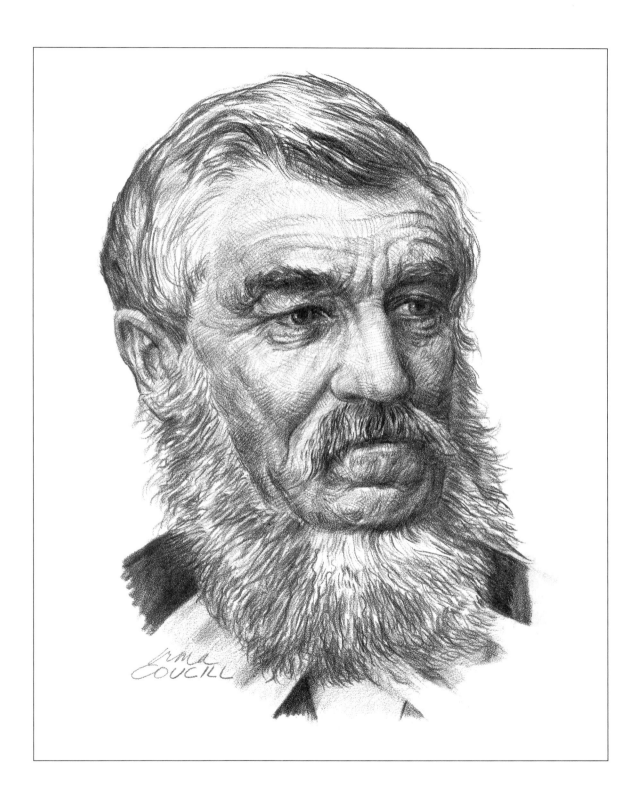

Index

Notice of Copyright